Expertise in Every Classroom

Expertise in Every Classroom

Guidelines to Bridging Research and Practice

Amanda Shuford Mayeaux and
Dianne F. Olivier

ROWMAN & LITTLEFIELD
Lanham • Boulder • New York • London

Published by Rowman & Littlefield
An imprint of The Rowman & Littlefield Publishing Group, Inc.
4501 Forbes Boulevard, Suite 200, Lanham, Maryland 20706
www.rowman.com

6 Tinworth Street, London SE11 5AL, United Kingdom

Copyright © 2020 by Amanda Shuford Mayeaux and Dianne F. Olivier

All rights reserved. No part of this book may be reproduced in any form or by any electronic or mechanical means, including information storage and retrieval systems, without written permission from the publisher, except by a reviewer who may quote passages in a review.

British Library Cataloguing in Publication Information Available

Library of Congress Cataloging-in-Publication Data Available

Library of Congress Control Number: 2020932583

ISBN 978-1-4758-5281-3 (cloth: alk. paper)
ISBN 978-1-4758-5282-0 (pbk.: alk. paper)
ISBN 978-1-4758-5283-7 (electronic)

This book is dedicated to the memory of Jan Wendling, expert teacher and friend, and to all of the expert teachers and leaders, who are changing the lives of students every day. If we all rock the boat, the ocean will move.

Contents

Acknowledgments	ix
Introduction	x
SECTION I. WHY EXPERT TEACHERS MATTER	**1**
1 Defining Expert Teachers	3
2 The Impact of Expert Teachers	13
3 The Why: Teacher-Student Kinship	20
SECTION II. THE THINKING PROCESSES OF EXPERT TEACHERS	**37**
4 The Expert Lens	39
5 The Expert Teacher Thinking Processes	48
6 Creating Conceptual Mastery	60
7 Learning Segments	71
8 The Day-to-Day	84
SECTION III. BUILDING EXPERT CAPITAL	**105**
9 Expert Capital within Schools	109
10 Professional Kinship	119
11 Collective Expert Thinking Process	126

Final Thoughts 134
Appendix: Professional Learning Activities 135
References 141
About the Authors 143

Acknowledgments

Amanda would like to thank her family, particularly her husband, who makes coffee and laughter a daily part of her writing process. She would also like to thank her mother, Jacque Shuford, her first teacher and mentor, who read the drafts and gave feedback and has cheered her through every step of her journey. Amanda would also like to acknowledge her own expert teacher professional learning community and their continued support of this work. Most of all, Amanda would like to thank Dianne for constantly refining and extending this important work. Experts develop experts.

Dianne would like to thank her husband and family, especially her five grandchildren, for their continued understanding of the time she devotes to her doctoral students and research. She would also like to thank Amanda for the opportunity as her chair to have observed her growth and transition from expert teacher to inquisitive doctoral student, to energetic university faculty member, as well as observed her maintaining a high level of expertise throughout the transitions. Dianne is excited to watch as Amanda continues to blossom.

Finally, this book would not have been possible without the amazing support of our peers at the University of Louisiana at Lafayette. From Dean Nathan Roberts to each person in our college and Educational Foundations and Leadership Department, we are thankful.

We are also thankful for all of our students, past, present, and future, who continue to push us to further refine our expertise. You are the reason we seek answers.

Introduction

"If you can dream it, you can do it." Walt Disney

Mrs. Van den Bosch was Amanda's first-grade teacher in the American School of Great Yarmouth, England. The class consisted of ten students. Amanda was a handful. Mrs. Van den Bosch had knee-length hair, which she wore in a bun on top of her head. As a reward for working quietly, not reading through lessons, and not bossing her classmates, she would let Amanda brush her hair during rest time.

"I loved to brush her hair. I hated rest time. Instead of punishing me, she developed me. I stopped reading through math. I stopped daydreaming as much. I participated. I loved school. She pondered the *why* of my behavior before finding the *how* solution. Forty plus years later, I remember her smell and her smile. I can draw out our classroom and describe many of the lessons. She was the first encounter I had with an expert or as I like to think of them, magical teachers. I have been intrigued ever since."

BACKGROUND

In the spring of 2006, Amanda along with her teaching partners, Monique Wild and Kathryn Edmonds, won the Middle School Teacher of the Year and the Overall Disney Teacher of the Year Awards. The Disney Awards were the bookend to her classroom career and she moved into administration the following January. Upon beginning her doctoral journey, she connected with Dianne, who was and is a professor at the University of Louisiana at Lafayette. Amanda asked Dianne to be her dissertation chair due to Dianne's profound and internationally known expertise of teaching and learning and research on professional learning communities. In the midst of Amanda's search for a dissertation topic, Dianne suggested she consider writing about expert teachers. Thus began our pursuit to understand the motivation, actions, and thinking processes of these outliers in education. This book is a culmination of the original research study (Mayeaux 2013), our personal experiences as and with experts, and our ongoing work with these educators.

The original study focused on a group of expert teachers, who were all national award–winning educators. They were diverse geographically, by grade level, and in the traditional areas of diversity, including age, race, gender, religion, and culture. The majority were found to be deeply humble people, who shared that they were not exceptional or unique, simply passionate about teaching and learning. When asked about their practice, most began sharing weaknesses and had to be redirected to share their strengths. All were hypersensitive about their students and their beliefs about teaching and learning.

PURPOSE

The purpose of the book is to offer a research-grounded, practitioner-focused model of expert educators to refocus educational reform efforts on the importance of recruiting, developing, and refining expertise in classrooms and schools across the nation. For too many years, reform efforts have focused primarily on standardizing assessments and curricula. While these efforts hold importance, these are not the true difference makers in the education of children. Overwhelming research continually undergirds the fact that the teacher is the single most important school-based factor impacting student achievement. The impact of an expert is exponential upon a student's success. Imagine an educational journey where a child has an expert in every class, every day, year after year!

WHO WILL USE THIS BOOK

Expertise in Every Classroom is for educators at all levels. This book has both research and practitioner elements. We believe that those seeking expertise desire both. The disconnect between research and practice is one of the barriers to the education profession becoming a true profession. Expert teachers are both academic researchers and critical practitioners. This book builds a bridge between research and practice, as we seek to open the doors between both groups.

At the teacher level, this book is for teachers, at any level, who are seeking to develop their expertise. Preservice and novice teachers should use this book to build a foundational understanding of expertise and to build in processes early in their careers that will lead to expertise. Experienced teachers may use this book to redefine and refine their current practices. The processes within this book are designed to guide practitioners through thinking processes that will further develop their skills, knowledge, and processes as they seek to develop toward expertise.

For leadership from the school to national levels, the book is designed to create and define a clear vision of expertise. One of the issues found in our research was that leaders struggle to recognize, support, and develop expertise. There was a consistent sentiment of expertise being dismissed. If we are to create a profession of experts, leadership at all levels must have a clear vision of expertise and the skills to build processes that develop it in all educators. Therefore, the book is also designed to support professional learning efforts in the development toward expertise at all levels.

Finally, we believe that the academic community must make research accessible and user friendly to practitioners. We also believe practitioners should be at the forefront of research discussions, sharing with academics their questions and practical issues, as well as being active participants in the work. Blending the ivory towers of academia with the daily work in our schools is how we can create a world class system for all students.

APPLICATION

Expertise in Every Classroom may be read individually or as part of a learning experience with a professional learning group or class. The book is designed to push readers to think like an expert by using reflection strategies and processes. These elements are built into the book to support the understanding and development of expertise at all levels.

Expertise in Every Classroom is divided into three distinct sections: section I: "Why Expert Teachers Matter," section II: "The Thinking Processes of Expert Teachers," and section III: "Building Expert Capital." Each section contains an introduction with a Thinking Questions section to be considered before, during, and after reading the section. Additionally, each chapter ends with Points to Ponder, which can be used for individual reflection and/or group discussions.

Throughout the chapters, Expert Vignettes have been added to share a practical perspective on the discussion. These vignettes are from expert teachers from around the country. The names of the experts have been changed to protect the teachers' identity. Readers will also find warnings about experts titled: Note of Caution. These sections are designed to allow the reader to understand the potential issues experts may present.

Readers will also find a list of professional learning activities included in the Appendix. These are designed to be used within professional learning teams and larger professional learning communities.

VISION

In our ongoing research of experts, we continue to focus on teachers and have broadened the work to examine expert leadership. As experts are in constant pursuit of improvement, we constantly seek to better understand experts, their teaching practices, their own knowledge, and their motivation. Our vision is to create a network of expert educators in efforts to build a grassroots reform initiative, where the best of the best work together with political entities and the public to rebuild a profession where experts are the norm and the reality in every classroom for every student, every day. Let the revolution begin!

Section I

WHY EXPERT TEACHERS MATTER

The secret to improving education is no mystery. Read any research report. Study any classroom where forgotten children have almost miraculously achieved goals once considered impossible. Talk to the homeless, forgotten student, who is now pursuing a degree. Behind many of these stories will be a teacher or a small group of teachers who went above and beyond to change the lives of students.

Beyond the research, each person can name that special teacher who made a profound difference in our lives. People smile when they remember that teacher, who sprinkled pixie dust on their heads and gave them a vision of our future. Often people enter education because of such a teacher, but many fail to develop such expertise.

Failure is due to multiple issues found entrenched in the teaching profession as a whole. First, the profession has evolved from an industrial mind-set of student production with teachers as the factory workers installing their part of the product. In the "factory," all workers are the same and the work is standardized and automated.

Elements of this mind-set are evident in the push for scripted lessons and low-level memorization software often found in schools. Second, the public perception and support of the teaching profession grow more and more negative each year, thus impacting the recruitment and retention of high-potential teachers. Finally, educators are in a constant struggle within the ranks between maintaining the *status quo* and reform.

The focus of this section is to create a foundation for understanding experts. Chapter 1, "Defining Expert Teachers," helps the reader create a holistic understanding of expert teachers and their skills, knowledge, and processes. Chapter 2, "The Impact of Expert Teachers," furthers outlines and supports the impact expert teachers have upon students and upon their learning communities. Finally, chapter 3, "The Why: Teacher-Student Kinship," sets forth the pivotal foundation upon which all experts build their relationships with students and which motivates them toward the constant development of expertise.

SECTION I: THINKING QUESTIONS

- Who was your favorite teacher? What characteristics, actions, and practices made this teacher special to you?
- What motivates you to develop as a professional?
- How do you define expertise in teaching? What is the evidence you would use to support your definition?
- What about the teaching profession supporting the development of expertise?
- What about the teaching profession undermining the development of expertise?

Chapter 1

Defining Expert Teachers

During her first six weeks of the year, Ms. Brown, a first-year teacher in a school with 100 percent poverty and 100 percent students of color, frequently considered running away from her job. She taught in a room with a weak projector and had to use her own laptop. Her dry erase board was so scratched and stained that it was useless. There was little to no resources, save a few old textbooks. She made and personally paid for every single activity in which the students participated, requiring plenty of after-school hours and quite a bit of money.

One day in late September, she decided to seek assistance from her instructional mentor with the aim of improving her practice and impacting students. Her mentor gave her a few resources, including books about effective teaching, videos of highly effective instruction, and also modeled and co-taught lessons in Ms. Brown's classroom. In turn, Ms. Brown videotaped her lessons and analyzed them with her mentor. She broke down her curriculum from the back to the front and realigned her lessons.

Ms. Brown spent six weeks mastering a few student-engagement strategies. She modeled these daily for her students and gave feedback until the students could use them perfectly. She reorganized the learning spaces based on student need. She created routines and rituals. All of the fall semester, she refined her teaching. In the spring, she pushed students harder than "those kids" had ever been pushed. She gave purposeful feedback and demanded that every child meet the state standard on every assignment, every day.

Her dedication to overcoming obstacles was decidedly demonstrated in her students' standardized test scores, as well as their notes of love to her at the end of the year. The group scored 11 percent proficient during their previous year on their statewide assessment, but after attending Ms. Brown's class the proficiency rate jumped to 67 percent for the same group of children on the state assessment. On her state teacher value-added report card, Ms. Brown was in the top 99 percent of teachers in the state for the value-added gains their students had achieved. The notes from her students were the true evidence and included comments like "No one has ever believed in me like you do" and "I never knew I was smart until you told me."

EXPERT TEACHERS

The students' comments and their success are the part of the story that should give us all hope. The unfortunate part of the story is that few asked this teacher how she accomplished such a feat. Many of her peers congratulated her, but many scoffed and mocked her. Wisdom would suggest people would be begging for her secrets. Sadly, her school leader even suggested she may not be retained the following year, because she did things a little too out of the box for his taste. He was also concerned that her students' success made other teachers uncomfortable.

She is not the only teacher with amazing results. Yet the story is the same for so many of these experts. *Effective teaching* can be learned and translated into student success. It is more elusive. Expertise is not based on years of experience or college degrees. Ms. Brown was a first-year teacher without a traditional education degree. She had a direct impact on students often dismissed by more experienced teachers. Her expertise was developed and continues to be developed, but, all too often, her work has caused many issues among peers and leadership.

RECOGNITION OF EXPERTS

The teaching profession is primarily a private affair. Teachers are locked away safely in their classrooms. Except for the occasional observation by administrators, the only people witnessing the teacher's actions are the students. Teachers seldom observe their peers and most assume whatever is happening in their classroom is the norm in all classrooms.

The pool of expert teachers for the initial study was composed of national award–winning teachers. The majority described negative responses from administration and peers for the recognition of their teaching. Interestingly, the experts were often confused by this response. Many stated they were fortunate, but any number of their peers were equally deserving. In many schools, this may be true, but in many others, there is a complete lack of recognition of expertise and a prevailing assumption that the expert teachers' successes are due simply to luck, rather than expertise.

The overarching consensus is all teachers are the same and all classrooms are the same. Most expert teachers thought they were really the norm at their schools. The shameful secret is behind closed doors: school leaders know the truth, but fear what acknowledging this truth would do. Teaching has an inherent characteristic of maintaining everyone is equal.

One school leader explained to an expert that her award made other teachers feel bad and that the expert should not mention it at school. He explained everyone worked hard and should be treated equally. There is some truth in the statement that others are working hard, but the expert is working differently and more effectively. To refuse to recognize this fact prevents our profession from improving and from leveraging the expertise.

THE TEACHING PROFESSION

Teaching has been described as crabs in the bucket profession. Like crabs, all teachers are considered the same. If anyone dares to start climbing out of the bucket, the job of the rest of the group is to pull them back down into the pile. The big secret in every school is everyone knows the truth: all teachers are not equal. In the quietness of hallways, there are whispers. Pushy parents know how to snag certain teachers for their children. Administrators know how to limit the issues caused by some teachers and use the more effective teachers to help students. Educational organizations undergird this premise by supporting and protecting all teachers. Political entities use this knowledge to paint all teachers and the system as ineffective.

If our educational system is to be truly reformed, the secret keeping must end and the consequences of years of neglecting to develop a profession of experts must be accepted. Through experience and research, the conclusion is that the teaching profession falls out into roughly five levels of experienced teachers: Expert; Highly Effective Teachers; Effective Teachers; No Harm-No Gain Teachers; and Do Harm Teachers (see figure 1.1).

HIGHLY EFFECTIVE TEACHERS AND EFFECTIVE TEACHERS

Much has been written about the highly effective teachers and effective teachers. Effective schools are staffed primarily with these teachers. They are motivated and hardworking. These two levels push students to grow and they understand teaching and learning.

Highly Effective Teachers' students exceed expected academic gains and social/emotional gains. These teachers build strong relationships with

Expert		Students exceed academic expectations, increase in learning habits, extremely positive growth in social/emotional skills. Experts crave and engage in professional learning. Potential positive impact on school culture.
	Highly Effective	Students exceed or meet academic expectations, increase somewhat in learning skills, and positively grow in social/emotional skills. Teachers seek and participate in professional learning. Positive impact on school culture.
	Effective	Students meet academic expectations, limited growth in life-long learning habits and social/emotional skills. Teachers participate in required professional learning. Positive impact on school culture.
Expected Impact		
	No Harm, No Gain	Students do not gain or may experience minimal regression academically. No impact on learning habits and social/emotional skills. Sit quietly through professional learning. Negative impact on school culture.
	Do Harm	Students regress significantly academically. Extreme negative impact on students learning habits and social/emotional well-being. Purposefully disrupt professional learning and negatively impact school culture.

Figure 1.1   The Impact of the Teaching Profession

students and with their families. They understand their students' needs and seek the students' success. These teachers embrace professional learning but do not necessarily seek it beyond the confines of their schools and districts. They are often on the brink of expertise but limited by their professional learning. These teachers will often seek and perform well in instructional leadership roles, as they are consistent and loyal.

Effective Teachers' students meet expected academic gains and have a slightly positive impact on their social/emotional development. They have pleasant relationships with students but limited contact with families. These teachers participate in professional learning and may use some new strategies but prefer the *status quo* in their classroom. They believe what they have been doing is effective and do not see a reason to develop new strategies. These teachers are often the backbone of the extracurricular activities at the school and serve as club sponsors and work after-school events. These are hardworking teachers, who believe in their school but not in their own need to develop past the effective level.

The veteran teachers from these two levels are willing to accept mandates pushed down on them with little pushback. They may be frustrated with scripted curricula and over-testing but, outside of a few comments, will not complain. They do not want to cast a negative light on their school and may fear political retribution. Many senior teachers are looking toward retirement and will work in this system until they can leave. The novice teachers manage or leave the profession.

THE DIRTY SECRETS OF EDUCATION

Little is written or discussed about the two lower levels. Often ineffective schools are staffed with novice teachers seeking a way out or with the lowest two levels of teachers on the ladder. Teacher unions' and organizations' unwillingness to acknowledge and manage these two lower levels has overshadowed their positive efforts. These teachers exist and in many hard-to-staff schools they are the majority. School leaders use strategies to contain them, because dismissal is almost impossible.

No Harm, No Gain Teachers' students experience academic gain. These teachers do not understand pedagogy or how to develop learning habits in their students. They are often the *fun* teachers or the *worksheet masters* in the school. There is little to no impact on the social/emotional development of students. These teachers participate in required professional learning but are often unable to understand and apply new strategies. No Harm, No Gain teachers are easily contained in places like nonessential electives or managing rote remediation programs. They manage computer labs or remain hidden with struggling students whose parents will not complain. These teachers, often perceived as "fun" teachers, are pliable and nice. Their classrooms are pretty but purposeless. Their students will complete projects, which are essentially academic fluff.

The other type is the worksheet masters known for the excessive amounts of mindless work they give students. The worksheets pile up by their desks with little purpose except for a grade. These teachers can often be found sitting at their desks passing the time, while students work on mindless work or chat. These teachers are nice and usually no one wants to hurt their feelings, so they are allowed to continue making copies, sitting at their desk, and simply passing the time.

The *Do Harm Teachers* are the least discussed of all and then only in hushed tones. Students in their classes not only regress academically, but, more importantly, experience extremely negative impact on their social/emotional development. These teachers are cruel and consistently provoke students. They boast of "not being afraid to fail kids" or "Back in my day, we could paddle that out of them." They are particularly adept at finding weaknesses in students and using these weaknesses to manipulate and intimidate students.

These teachers resist all forms of professional learning. They are aggressive and bully other teachers and the leadership. They leverage their political affiliations and their ability to call their lawyer to control others. They undermine peers and effective school leaders. They are oppositional in their dealings with parents. Failure is always blamed on "those kids," the curriculum, the parents, the school, the lack of resources, and the like. They are never at fault. Their social media posts underscore how dreadful everything is in education. They are toxic, both in their classrooms and in their schools. They are allowed to remain.

Every school has a few of them. They lower the level of performance of students and the overall effectiveness of the school. Everyone in the school community knows who they are. The school administration works to hide them where they can do the least amount of harm, but when they do harm, the administration will protect them, in order not to be the top news story or suffer politically. These teachers come in direct conflict with the three highest levels and often try to entice the No Harm, No Gain crew onto their side.

THE EXPERT LEVEL

The *Expert Level* is primarily unrecognized, and limited understanding exists in the practitioner world about these educators. In the research world, multiple studies have examined the practices of these outliers (Berliner 2004; Darling-Hammond 1995; Good and Brophy 2008; Hattie 2003; Marzano 2010). Hattie (2003, 5) summarizes the overall understanding that "expert teachers can identify essential representations of their subject, can guide learning through classroom interactions, can monitor learning and provide feedback, can attend to affective attributes, and can influence student outcomes. These five major dimensions lead to 16 prototypic attributes of expertise. Herein lie the differences."

Defining and understanding these dimensions is critical in the research, but in order to create a profession where experts are the norm rather than the outliers means communicating expert research into language and skills practitioners can apply in their own professional learning. Students of expert teachers exceed academic expectations. Students also develop and increase highly effective learning habits that impact them throughout their lives. Finally, experts have a profound and extremely positive growth on the social and emotional well-being of their students. These all combine to create what the expert considers *conceptual mastery* of the whole student.

The initial study (Mayeaux 2013) was created to understand what motivates a person to develop toward expertise. Findings showed expert teachers are motivated by their relationship with their students and their ability to make positive change in the lives of their students. This factor is defined as Teacher-Student Kinship (chapter 3). Of all the elements that describe experts, this is the one element that cannot be taught. Every decision from classroom action to professional learning choices hinges on the context of their students. The Teacher Expert Motivation Framework is a model of the expert teacher (Mayeaux 2013) (see figure 1.2).

Teacher-Student Kinship is a familial type of relationship between students and expert teachers. The relationship is the core of the teacher's motivation to develop expertise and is grounded in the teacher's overwhelming sense of responsibility to impact not only students' mastery of content, but more importantly students' learning habits and social/emotional development well

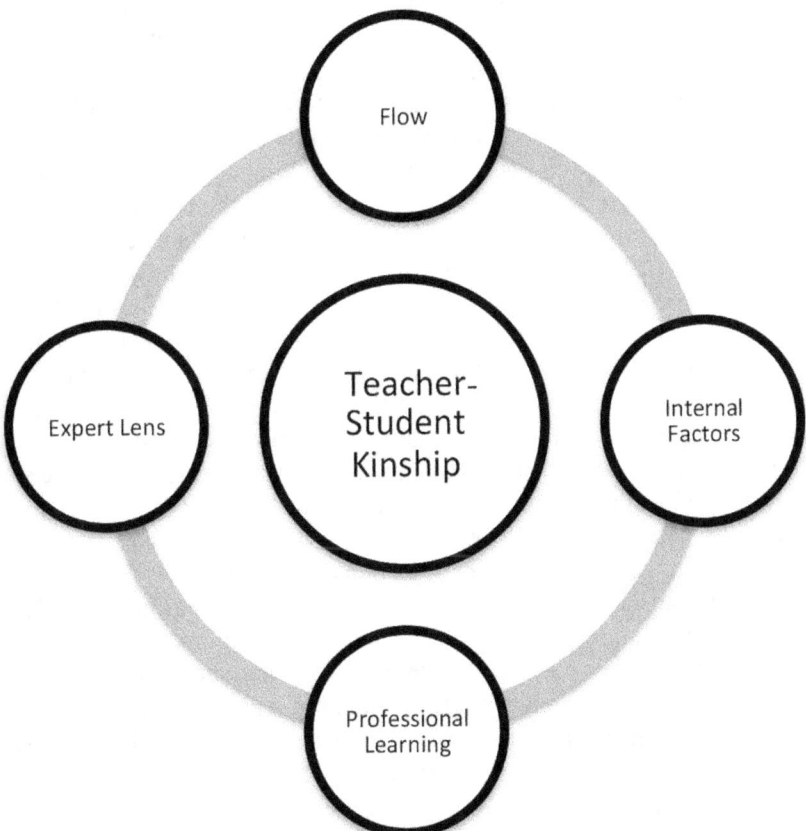

Figure 1.2 The Expert Teacher Motivation Framework *Source*: Mayeaux, Amanda. 2013. "Motivating Teachers towards Expertise Development: A Mixed-Methods Study of the Relationships between School Culture, Internal Factors, and State of Flow." Lafayette: University of Louisiana at Lafayette.

past their time with the teacher. All other elements revolve around this central motivator.

Expert Lens is the viewpoint of the expert teacher to apply all three types of highly developed skills, pedagogical, content, and interpersonal, into a single focused lens in order to make decisions concerning teaching and learning for each individual student. The ability is based on the teacher's strong internal factors, as well as one's strong pedagogical, content, and social-emotional attributes. These seamlessly merge together to create a lens through which all teacher decisions are based from the classroom to their professional learning choices.

Professional Learning is the professional learning experience expert teachers choose for themselves. Experts crave professional learning. Their choices are based on specific needs they see in their teaching and are directly related to their perceived weaknesses in order to improve their own craft and thereby improve their students' achievement. Expert teachers are motivated by deep-impacting professional learning. Expert teachers seek high-functioning professional learning experiences. Experts are often reclusive in schools, unless paired with other experts or, at minimum, highly effective teachers. If their school meets their expectations, they are more willing to participate; however, if the school culture is subpar to their expectations, the teachers will create their own professional mini-culture within or outside of their school.

Flow is the mental state of operation where a person is fully immersed in an activity and experiences a feeling of extreme energized focus, complete involvement, and success in the activity, or, simply explained, completely focused motivation (Csikszentmihalyi 1990). Expert teachers experience flow as they completely engage in single-minded immersion into teaching and learning. Experts embrace teaching and working with students despite obstacles and often will work with more difficult students to experience even greater Flow. The expert teacher's experience of Flow is tied directly to the Teacher-Student Kinship they have developed with the students.

Internal Factors, as defined by Costa and Garmston (2001), include efficacy, craftsmanship, flexibility, interdependence, and consciousness. These factors increase and decrease based on external situations and experiences. The individual factors play highly into individual motivation and persistence. Expert teachers are extremely reflective thinkers, who seek to highly develop these five human passions in order to meet the needs of their students, in order to experience flow, and to ultimately further develop the Teacher-Student Kinship. Experts also develop these factors in their students.

UNDERSTANDING THE EXPERTS

Once we understand that teaching is an art and a science, logic would suggest both can be developed and improved. While some teachers embrace growth through professional learning, experts purposefully and obsessively seek it. Education is one of the only professions where expertise is not only shunned but such knowledge is purposefully ignored as a method of improvement. When a child has an expert teacher, the difference is clear and the impact almost immediate. Yet experts are consistently ignored. Understanding the experts means moving past classroom actions to what motivates the experts' constant and obsessive pursuit of excellence.

One of the elements practitioners of education often resist is research and the way it is developed. On the flipside, academics often resist the practitioners' experiences. The key to understanding expert teachers and the rest of this book is to understand the simultaneous interplay between the foundational research and practitioners' experiences. To ignore either would be to present a simplified version of a complex phenomenon. To appeal only to researchers is to suggest that practitioners' experiences are invalid. To appeal only to practitioners is to suggest that the research is too complex and uninteresting. To revolutionize this profession, both must be woven together into one understanding.

THE EXPERT TEACHER EXPLAINED

The discussion throughout this book concerns the individual elements used to describe expert teachers. However, readers are strongly cautioned to remember expertise is developed through the interconnectivity of these elements. The purpose of dissecting and discussing each element in isolation is to provide the foundation the reader needs to critically understand and apply the elements as a cohesive whole.

The expert teacher as a whole is one who develops, maintains, and maximizes the Teacher-Student Kinship. This element is the driving motivational force behind a teacher's pursuit to purposefully and consistently polish their Expert Lens. The experts are hyperaware of each of the sub-lenses, pedagogical, content, and interpersonal knowledge, but seamlessly merge these together to analyze the why behind each interaction in the classroom. When they encounter issues that may prove beyond their current expertise, they will purposefully seek professional learning specific to their context.

NOTE OF CAUTION

Expert teachers have been shown to function at high capacity, regardless of school culture; however, they also prefer an optimal school culture of shared leadership, strong differentiated professional learning, and positive collegial relationships. While experts have great potential to positively impact school culture, they are often reclusive in schools, unless paired with other experts or, at minimum, highly effective teachers. If their school meets their expectations, they are more willing to participate; however, if the school culture is subpar to their expectations, the teachers will create their own professional mini-culture within or outside of their school. Experts are very territorial of their students and their classrooms. They desire purposeful feedback from peers and leadership they trust. They also will resist any program, curriculum, strategy, or professional learning they deem, based on evidence, to be unbeneficial to their students.

In our study, experts consistently shared beliefs that teaching was their "calling" or "vocation" and their students' success was their purpose in life. Many choked up when discussing difficult situations and laughed gleefully when discussing successes. Understanding the conceptual picture of these outliers allows teachers and leaders seeking expertise a window into how to continuously grow and leadership insight into how to recognize, recruit, retain, refine, and build upon such magic.

POINTS TO PONDER

- All teachers do not teach at the same level of effectiveness. The overarching refusal of the system to accept this fact creates barriers in the profession that limit the development of expertise.
- Teacher-Student Kinship is the motivational foundation pushing experts to consistently and constantly persist toward expertise.

Chapter 2

The Impact of Expert Teachers

Simply stated, the educational community knows everything needed to revolutionize the teaching profession and build an education system to positively impact every student. The facts clearly illustrate that students with benefits, such as engaged, educated, and financially stable families, have a better chance at success than students without stable, educated, and financially secure homes. However, rather than focusing on factors the school is unable to change, the secret to success is focusing on the number one factor that schools do control that impacts student achievement: teachers.

Knowing how and actually changing the system have proven to be two very different issues. The walls against change are so entrenched in the system that the majority of efforts to reform education have failed. Billions of dollars are spent each year on programs, testing, curricula, and professional learning. Yet little has changed in the U.S. education system.

Antiquated structures from salary scales to professional learning have withstood any sort of innovation. The private sector's attempt to invade through vouchers and charter schools has been suicidal at best as high levels of corruption for profit and quick-fix programs have led to the lack of stamina and sustainability. In all of the chatter, the discussion has seldom focused on finding and strategically learning from experts. Reform efforts have ignored proven structures and strategies used internationally to improve the teaching profession. In fact, expert outliers often experience shunning from their peers and leadership.

In 2012, The New Teacher Project released the study *The Irreplaceables*, about a group of teachers who were so successful in producing high student achievement that replacing them would be an almost impossible task (TNTP

2012). These teachers were described as creating more engaging learning experiences for students, who then reached achievement gains of five to six more months of learning each year than students of low-performing teachers. Common sense would lead us to believe that these teachers were highly sought after for teaching positions, leading professional learning, and mentoring novice teachers.

Common sense could not be further from the truth. Rather, the study shared that only 37 percent of these high-performing teachers' administrators encouraged them to remain at their school and in the teaching profession. Additionally, the turnover rate for Irreplaceables was over 50 percent. The Irreplaceables cited the following multiple reasons for leaving:

- poor school culture;
- poor working conditions;
- standardized compensation structures prevented any type of financial incentives to retain these teachers;
- consistent lack of differentiation from leadership for high-performing and low-performing teachers;
- limited recognition of high performance;
- little to no encouragement to share opportunities or paths for teacher leadership roles; and
- shockingly, 6 percent or more of low performers were encouraged to seek leadership roles.

Forty years of research and over twenty-five years of reform models have led to few changes in the teaching profession. Both national and international research demonstrates that expertise in teaching can be clearly defined and developed. Countries, such as Finland, Canada (Ontario), and Singapore, have successfully revamped their systems to develop and support expert teachers (Darling-Hammond and Rothman 2011). The problem is a dependable and credible way to solidly connect achievement effects to teacher effects. While value-added models are being used across the country, the linkage to single achievement test scores leaves out the impact teachers have upon the student's self-efficacy, self-concept, and possible future motivation to learn.

Yet some teachers overcome all the barriers and develop expertise. These teachers find avenues of development either in small pockets of peers or individually. While countries, as demonstrated by Darling-Hammond and Rothman (2011), are developing experts in mass numbers, the United States is only randomly and haphazardly creating such teachers. The first step in creating more experts is recognizing that they exist.

THE IMPACT OF EXPERT TEACHERS

Research has proved that of the educational elements within the control of the school system, the quality of the teacher has by far had the most positive impact on student achievement (Rivkin, Hanushek, and Kain 2005; Rockoff 2004; Sanders and Rivers 1996). Expert teachers strongly and positively impact the whole student's development and not just the academic element. Expert teachers aim to surpass academic achievement goals to also strongly and positively impact students' lifelong learning skills and social-emotional attributes, thus developing Conceptual Mastery of the student. Teacher-Student Kinship pushes experts to have a lifelong impact on the students, as this relationship is the foundation for all motivation toward expertise.

Academic Impact

> *I run my classroom.... It is strict you know, I have rules and I expect the kids to abide by them but my overarching goals is that... they realize that hard work pays off and then their education is important. Other teachers were like, "Why do you do all that? Why don't you just put a zero in the grade book and be done with it?" I just can't do that. I have to feel like those kids are getting the most out of their education because nobody can take that education away from them and I think they see that I really value them as individuals and their education and also I'm not just going to throw in the towel and say, "Well if you don't want to do your homework then that's your problem."* (Sandy, high school math teacher)

Research continually confirms, study after study, that high teacher quality impacts gains in learning across classrooms, even when compared within the same school. Some teachers consistently demonstrate greater student achievement gains than other teachers. For example, two students starting at the same level of achievement can know vastly different amounts at the end of a single academic year based solely on the effectiveness of the teacher (Sanders and Rivers 1996). Also proven is the fact that poor teaching can lead to compounded issues. Poor teaching in students' early school career or in consecutive years leads to poor overall achievement, from which students may never recover (Sanders and Rivers 1996).

When examining expert teachers, the way they approach teaching and learning is clearly different from other teachers. Experts focus on why things are happening or not happening as opposed to quick-fix solutions. Experts do not rely on strategies pushed down from the district or school level to solve their students' issue. Experts are engaged minute by minute in solutions through the use of Nimble Feedback. Expert teachers set very high expectations, first, for themselves and then for their students (Good and Brophy 2008).

They believe and embrace the idea that their students' academic achievement is their responsibility. This belief is critical to the teachers' willingness to consistently reteach, supply critical feedback, research and apply new strategies, and communicate that they fully believe their students can learn (Good and Brophy 2008).

Expert teachers also constantly use action research to find out why students are struggling and they implement strategies to fix the issues. Additionally, they engage students in the action research process and solutions to create independent learners. While the expert has a clear set of academic goals, they understand goals are not exceeded by only focusing on the mastery of content knowledge. Experts are able to push students to exponential gains due in part to their focus on developing the students' ability to learn and their social/emotional well-being.

Impact on Learning Habits

> *If you want kids to get excited about learning, create a sense of curiosity . . . make them wonder. They love a good mystery.* (Mona, English teacher)

Expert teachers understand that learning is a lifelong endeavor often based in simple curiosity. Expert teachers develop students' understanding that learning is more than content knowledge, grades, and test scores. The various skills needed to be lifelong learners are integrated and practiced daily in the expert teacher's reflective classroom.

Expert teachers engage students in reflection practice concerning their learning. They help students set goals and reflect on their movement toward the goals. Expert teachers are tremendously adept problem solvers, who purposefully develop problem-solving skills, both academically and interpersonal, in their students. The expert teacher values creativity and encourages the development of students' tendencies to be creative by allowing students to develop and apply new ideas and solutions.

Expert teachers teach students *how to think*, rather than *what to think* through various strategies and processes. By using students' curiosity, expert teachers help them learn to seek, analyze, and evaluate information. Students are free to discover, discuss, and explore ideas and concepts to find answers to their curiosity-driven questions. The expert teacher grounds these items in the content.

Impact on Social-Emotional Attributes

"No matter what is thrown at me (in the clasroom) I can figure it out because Mrs. Jones (Johanne) taught me how to use the resources I have around me. She taught me how to use my strengths to find a job to interact with people. She taught me not to be afraid to ask for help or for questions." I just I want them (Johanne's students) to be able to find success in something but that they found success independently. That they are able to do it and have the confidence to go do it! (Johanne, high school science)

The most significant difference between expert teachers and highly effective teachers is the positive impact the expert has upon the students' social and emotional well-being. The expert teacher is a life-changer for students. This is due to the Teacher-Student Kinship being at the center of all of their interactions, choices, and actions. Expert teachers not only have highly developed social/emotional attributes but also have the ability to develop social/emotional attributes in students.

Expert teachers enhance students' self-concept (Covington 1998) and self-efficacy (Bandura 1993) about learning. They set appropriately challenging tasks to aim students toward both surface and deep outcomes with a focus not only on content mastery but also in building students' social-emotional attributes.

Students' self-efficacy is greatly impacted by an expert teacher through rigorous academic engagement. The experts' deep content and pedagogical knowledge allow them to create lessons that are specifically designed to teach students how to learn. Their high-honed social-emotional attributes create the culture where this type of reflective learning is encouraged and expected. Through this daily process, self-efficacy is increased as students experience success, while learning to overcome barriers.

Hattie (2003) states that one of the attributes of expert teachers is their ability to attend to affective attributes of students. This is due to their involvement and caring for the students, creating a picture of a teacher's willingness to be receptive to what the students need. Rather than attempting to dominate the situation, an expert teacher has a strong influence on student outcomes by increasing a student's self-efficacy, self-regulation, and willingness to be challenged.

Impact on Classroom Culture

I think that once they realize that I'm going to do different things for different kids, I think that kind of builds the culture a lot because they stop competing with each other and I feel like that's really important for them to feel like they're in it together. Now we can connect with, you know, all these people all over the world and then I hope that their gaining this idea that other people matter, even if they don't speak English, they still matter and we can learn from them and we can share ideas and you know connect. (Abby, middle school English)

Expert teachers create a classroom culture based on relationships and respect both between the teacher and the students and among the students. Hattie (2003) found expert teachers are also able to consistently optimize a classroom culture to be welcoming. Errors are expected and embraced as a springboard for teaching and learning. The students and teacher work together with a team mind-set that everyone should succeed. The students build relationships with the teacher and with each other that extend well beyond the school year. These relationships are grounded in trust and respect.

NOTE OF CAUTION

In many cases, expert teachers are embraced by peers and by school leaders. However, for the most part, the impact of expert teachers in their schools is limited by leadership and peers. Expert teachers often describe feeling isolated and misunderstood. Their obsessive need for professional learning through conversations is often misinterpreted by less-developed peers and seen as a threat by leadership.

I went into her room and I said this is kind of what I'm thinking but I don't know exactly how to put it together. . . . What would you do? And kind of tossed the verbal football back and forth for about twenty minutes and she gave me ideas and we talked it about it. . . . I implemented the lesson and it was just awesome and then mmm I was able to carry it out for several days and keep reflecting back on it and it was. I wasn't able to carry that out completely without her input and so when I have a person that's willing to share great ideas and listen to my ideas and help me it is awesome but unfortunately I don't get that very often with my teachers. (Ann, middle school)

While they crave the discussions, they recognize that, within the school, these could lead to difficulties with peers and leadership. Therefore, they seek professional learning outside of their schools and hide their expertise.

Section III, "Building Expert Capital," will focus on leveraging experts and their expertise to develop and grow expertise in schools. Understanding experts' perspectives is the key to unlocking their potential to have profound impact beyond their classrooms.

POINTS TO PONDER

- Expert teachers impact the whole student in profoundly positive ways.
- The impact has far-reaching ramifications and can change the trajectory of a student's life.
- Expert teachers crave rigorous professional learning focused on the needs of their students. They also desire to engage with peers for professional learning but often feel like outcasts.

Chapter 3

The Why: Teacher-Student Kinship

My advice to a younger person going into education . . . you have to realize that you've put lives in your hands and part of their future is your responsibility. (Kate, middle school English teacher)

WHY TEACHERS DEVELOP EXPERTISE

Teacher-Student Kinship is a familial-type relationship expert teachers have with their students. The relationship is the core of the expert teacher's motivation to develop expertise and is grounded in the teacher's overwhelming sense of responsibility to impact not only students' mastery of their content but also, more importantly, students' life past their time with the teacher. Teacher-Student Kinship is the single driving force motivating expert teachers to increase their skills and abilities in order to positively impact each student.

The art of teaching is very personal to expert teachers. These experts shoulder the responsibility of each child's success to a very deep and personal level. Their strong internal factors relate to the relationships they have with their students and the responsibility they feel toward them. Melissa, a high school math teacher, clearly defined the epitome of this relationship: "They have to trust you and that's basically starts with a relationship from day one you've got to get to know the kid, not just the kid, but where the kid is coming from and what the kid likes and what the kid doesn't like . . . what the kid's strengths and weaknesses are, interests are and know that relationship so they know that you're not just interested in whether they can multiply seven times eight and that's a problem, but you're interested in them as a person. You want them to succeed whether it is seven times eight or whether a baseball game."

Experts' greatest joy is when a troubled student achieves success. The stories shared demonstrated that teachers believe they have tremendous power to shape the lives of children and take the responsibility seriously. The teachers set high expectations and goals but also believe in their own ability to help the students succeed.

When asked to share advice for future teachers, Jane, a fifth-grade teacher, stated:

> Those kids who fight for success and you know that you can make a difference in their lives and we're . . . we're getting so many kids from just torn homes you know, when you feel like you're the only constant in their life that they can depend on you. Miss Jane will always be in room 98 from eight to four, I know that you know it's a constant.

Expert teachers focus beyond the content and the classroom to help students see the potential for their lives. Content mastery and classroom interactions are a tool in teaching students to realize their individual potential, rather than the focus. Expert teachers believe their relationships with the students does not begin and end with the school year. They believe they have the ability and responsibility to impact students for life.

PURPOSE OF TEACHER-STUDENT KINSHIP

The purpose of Teacher-Student Kinship is twofold. First, the expert teacher uses the relationship to truly and deeply develop a Whole Student Understanding of each student in the classroom. The understanding focuses on the whole student, including their strengths and weaknesses, in three overarching areas: content, learning habits, and social-emotional attributes. The goal for each student is to achieve Conceptual Mastery as a learner. Learners who achieve Conceptual Mastery are able to make connections across the content, between contents, leverage learning habits, and engage with others using strong social-emotional attributes.

Jan, a middle school teacher, explained:

> It's (the big idea) not even mathematical. It's more just about not giving up. I want kids to know that they don't have to be good at math to be good at math. I mean . . . too many kids come in with this idea of "Well I'm just not good at math," so then they think they're never going to be good. But that's . . . that doesn't have anything to do with it. It's about believing in themselves.
>
> Getting them to not give up and just working . . . the desire to work hard and have that perseverance and that pays off and if I can get the kids to believe in themselves and to know that I believe in them that they can do it then it doesn't

even matter what I teach them because they find it easy after that. You know because they don't always find it easy at first but they don't give up and then they get so much self-action when they do well. I have very few kids fail and I think it's because of that. I've tried to build them up all the time.

Second, Teacher-Student Kinship is the foundation upon which an expert experiences Flow (Csikszentmihalyi 1990), the complete immersion in the teaching and learning process.

The constant seeking to understand why issues exist and then finding solutions to benefit the student is extremely rewarding for the expert.

For example, experts do not see misbehavior as something that needs an intervention but rather something to explore and uncover the underlying reasons. Expert teachers believe the only way to overcome issues is to first understand why the issues exist. Understanding such issues at the level the expert requires is dependent on the student equally engaging in the exploration. Teacher-Student Kinship allows for such a symbiotic relationship of respect, trust, self-efficacy, and persistence. The expert consistently goes to great lengths to establish and reinforce this relationship with each student.

The ability to see the student as a whole means seeing not only their content knowledge needs but also their learning habit needs and interpersonal skill needs. The vision is a constant inner play between the Teacher-Student Kinship and the Expert Lens. Nonexperts focus on the external conditions from the lack of parental support to lack of resources when they consider the success or failure of students.

Due to their extremely high self-efficacy, experts focus on the students and truly believe in their own abilities to make change and students' abilities to grow. The expert not only knows and understands how to build powerful relationships so desired in Teacher-Student Kinship but also knows and understands how to change the student's knowledge, skills, strategies, and habits through their focusing and refocusing of the Expert Lens, which is the focus of section II.

WHOLE STUDENT UNDERSTANDING

The expert teacher focuses on developing Whole Student Understanding of each student. Whole Student Understanding aligns with the expert's Expert Lens (chapter 5). Understanding the whole student is a merger of three distinct elements the learner brings into the classroom (see figure 3.1).

Content mastery involves the student's mastery of content knowledge, skills, and processes of the content. In their development of Whole Student Understanding, experts analyze and evaluate students' prior mastery of the content by gathering multiple sources of evidence. As the year progresses,

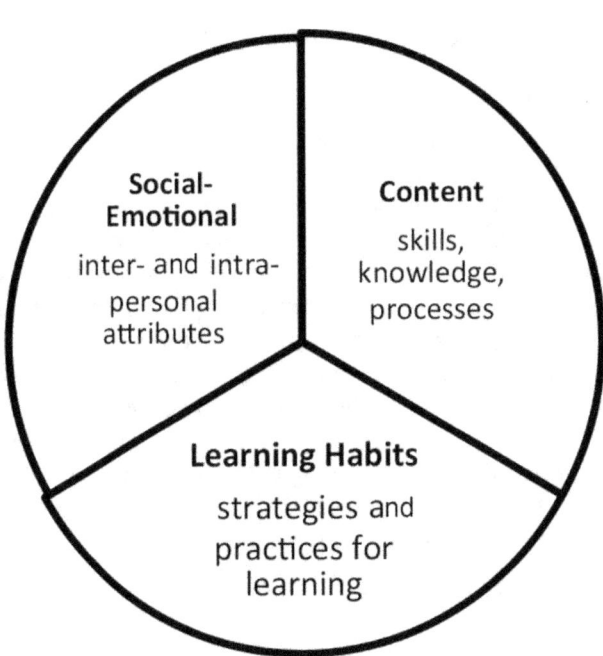

Figure 3.1   Elements of Whole Student Understanding

experts consistently seek evidence to help them deeply understand what students know and what they are able to do with proficiency. Experts also constantly engage students in the process of understanding what they do not know and work with them to develop their content mastery.

Learning Habits are the strategies and practices student use to learn. Experts do not view strategies as a simple rote practice to teach students to help them write better or remember the steps in solving a problem. Rather, experts view strategies as techniques to introduce, nurture, and develop students' ability to learn independently. Strategies become practices that are norms for the learner and carry through their life.

Social-Emotional Attributes are the interpersonal and intrapersonal attributes of the students. These wide-ranging attributes are critical to students being successful. These are often the attributes that cause students to falter in later educational pursuits. Interpersonal skills include such things as listening, respect, trust, kindness, team-work, problem-solving, negotiation skills, and conflict resolution. Intrapersonal skills include such things as self-efficacy, perseverance, flexibility, patience, self-motivation, and self-reflection. Experts build these in students as a class and as individuals. The expert's attention to this element of the whole student is key to their ability to build strong Teacher-Student Kinship.

TEACHER-STUDENT KINSHIP DECONSTRUCTED

"The manner used by the teacher to treat the students, respect them as learners and people, and demonstrate care and commitment for them are attributes of expert teachers" (Hattie 2003, 8).

Expert teachers attend consistently first and foremost to the affective attributes of their students. Experts are truly engaged in their students' presence in the classroom. Housner and Griffey (1985) found the number of requests for information made by expert and experienced teachers during the time they are planning instruction is about the same, but experts needed to know about the ability, experience, and background of the students they will teach. Teacher-Student Kinship is the power of the relationship between the teacher and the student (see figure 3.2). However, it carries over into the classroom culture as a whole and creates a powerful learning environment. Expert teachers understand this is the secret to all success with each student and these teachers are purposeful in the development of the relationship.

Respect

Respect is one of the critical elements in developing Teacher-Student Kinship. When discussing respect, many teachers will focus on the students'

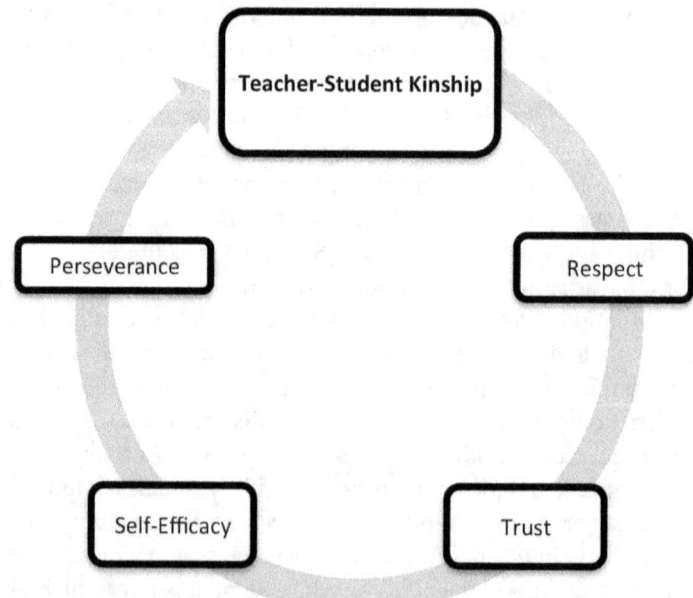

Figure 3.2 Teacher-Student Kinship

demonstration of respect toward the teacher. Nonexpert teachers create long lists of expectations that will demonstrate respect and then spend a great deal of time focusing on how the students correctly or incorrectly respond. Ineffective teachers waste hours of classroom time redirecting and dealing with disrespectful behavior.

Expert teachers approach the classroom differently. They begin the year demonstrating respect for each individual student and continue to consistently demonstrate respect for their students through their words and actions. This shift in mind-set produces tremendous benefits and is the starting point of the development of the other three elements: trust, self-efficacy, and persistence.

Expert teachers build respect in multiple ways, but the most important are the initial actions. First and foremost, experts treat all students professionally without favoritism or negativity. Expert teachers initiate the building of respect prior to students arriving to let them know the teacher is excited to have them as students. This may happen in the form of postcards home over the summer or a phone call prior to school starting. Expert teachers are very purposeful in making positive connections with both the student and their families prior to school beginning to create a foundation of respect.

On the first day of school, the expert teacher's classroom is student-friendly and ready for learners. The teacher may have something a little special for the students on their desks, which could be anything from a nice pencil to a quick survey. The expert warmly greets each student at the door, with a smile, and welcomes them specifically.

The rest of the day is not about "laying down the law" but rather about building the foundations of the classroom culture. The expert will have students introduce themselves in a fun manner. The students may participate in some icebreakers and the teacher will consistently reinforce the positives. By the end of the class or day, students will have produced something to add to the classroom and will leave with some sort of positive note home. The expert consistently demonstrates respect for all students.

The first few weeks are about getting to know each and every student personally. The expert teachers take the time to get to know their students through surveys, team-building activities, face-to-face conversations, chats on the way to lunch, or quick little positive comments about the students' work or behavior.

Quickly the expert understands a quirk of the eyebrow is a sign of frustration of one student, but of confusion on another. They know which child needs a little extra time to cool down after recess than another. Experts know their students' needs, likes, dislikes, and leverage these to model respect. When observing the experts, they are constantly moving among and interacting with the students.

Modeling respect for students through their actions toward the students is a secret skill experts have, which can be transferred to the highly effective teachers and effective teachers. The modeling of respect has to be purposeful, positive, and persistent.

Trust

Trust is the second critical element in developing Teacher-Student Kinship. Many students come to school with trust issues. Trust is the belief students have concerning how the teacher will fairly leverage their power in the classroom. Expert teachers understand how past and current experiences may impact a student's ability to develop trust, particularly the marginalized students. Tschannen-Moran (2014, p. 19–20) defines trust as "willingness to be vulnerable to another based on the confidence that the other is benevolent, honest, open, reliable and competent."

Expert teachers do small things to build trust. Experts are reliable. They show up, every day, prepared to teach well-planned, highly engaging lessons. While this sounds simple, many non-teachers do not take the time to prepare engaging lessons. This is far above simply writing a lesson plan; these lessons are grounded in the expert's elaborate planning and refinement of their teaching.

Experts demonstrate competence through consistency in their expectations and their abilities to grow the whole student. Experts make mistakes, but err on the side of the student. Experts accept responsibility when they make mistakes. Expert teachers apologize when they are wrong and forgive when they have been wronged. This openness creates openness in the classroom.

Experts demonstrate benevolence as they treat all students fairly, regardless of the students' prior reputation, race, gender, orientation, religion, political beliefs, economic status, and the like. An expert teacher may choose the most notorious student to take forms and money to the office on the first day of school. By doing so, the teacher is creating a paradigm shift for the student that this year will be different. Expert teachers do not play favorites in the classroom. Expert teachers ensure equity in all areas, but particularly equity in success. For example, if there is a project, no student will be penalized for not being able to afford a poster board or rewarded because the student's family could buy fancy lights for their science fair board.

Expert teachers focus on the positive and often ignore the little negatives. Experts are honest with students about where they are not only in the learning continuum but also in their deeply held belief that the student can be successful. Expert teachers give honest feedback with a strong dose of compassion and purpose. When correcting, they are direct and to the point but without judgment. They reinforce the positives, in order to overcome the obstacles.

An analysis of Ms. Brown's classes found she gave 143 positive comments in a ninety-minute period and every child received at least five or six per class period. Even when she had to give correction feedback for work, she began with the positives. The students then trusted the negative feedback and sought to improve.

Experts understand that judgment can be given through body language, facial expressions, and tone of voice. They manage their responses and control impulses to build trust. Students, in turn, reciprocate as trust builds upon respect. When experts believe in students and students begin to trust the new vision set before them, then students can accept the next two pieces of the Teacher-Student Kinship puzzle.

Self-Efficacy

Expert teachers are highly efficacious about their ability to reach all students, despite barriers. Their high self-efficacy is almost contagious as it begins to permeate the students' self-efficacy. Once there is respect and trust, the expert teacher begins to rebuild the students' vision of their abilities, potential, and goals for life by increasing the students' self-efficacy. The expert's high self-efficacy refuses to accept that students will not be able to overcome barriers.

However, this belief is not a pie-in-the-sky sort of idea but rather a catalyst to develop, implement, and refine concrete actions. The expert's self-efficacy is the reason the expert asks why before how. They need to understand the student, the barrier, and the issue before figuring out a plan of action. The expert understands the student must be an active participant in the process of understanding why. The student participates, because the student respects and trusts the teacher. This cycle is daily and the self-efficacy grows in the student.

Persistence

The final element of the Teacher-Student Kinship is persistence. Expert teachers build upon the respect, trust, and self-efficacy elements to create the magical element in Teacher-Student Kinship, which is persistence. Experts develop persistence first through modeling the relationship to students in very personal ways. Experts share their own learning struggles, both current and previous. One middle school math expert teacher shared the F she earned in her first college math course, but then she shared the A she earned the second time she took the class.

Experts are honest about what they are learning and how it is impacting them as learners. Another teacher brought in all the things she was reading and discussed how she uses reading to learn things she needs to know.

Another shared how he sometimes watched videos to find better ways to teach things. After trying out a new method, he asked students for feedback about the lesson. He accepted the feedback and modified the strategy for the next class. His constant thinking aloud about how things were going in the class created a collaborative culture in the classroom.

Experts also persist when students are struggling. They focus on what is going well, rather than giving up. More importantly, they seek answers to why things are not working, as opposed to quick fixes. Their answer-seeking is not about a data point but rather about students. They talk to students and ask them what they are thinking, where they are struggling, and why the barriers exist.

Regardless of grade or content taught, when experts were asked, "What is the big picture concept you want your students to learn in your class?" every single respondent stated something concerning persistence.

- "I want my kids to know, there is nothing they can't overcome, if they don't give up." (Jeremiah, high school chemistry)
- "The big picture for me is learning to learn from failure as much as you learn from success and to keep going for your goals." (Fran, first grade)
- "My students learn quickly to fail forward. We work hard on giving and receiving feedback, understanding where they did not meet the mark, and how to overcome their weaknesses. This is persistence building and it is the most important thing I teach." (Jane, middle school)

Expert teachers use their finely honed expertise to push students to develop Conceptual Mastery as a learner. The expert understands while the quadratic formula may fade from a student's mind, the persistence learned through the mastering of the formula has lifelong implications.

HOW EXPERTS DEVELOP TEACHER-STUDENT KINSHIP

The beginning of any relationship is about first impressions. Expert teachers understand this concept and strategize to maximize the impact of this initial period. Expert teachers prefer receiving their class lists well before school begins. These lists are invaluable to the expert in making connections with students and their families during the summer through various types of activities.

Experts view families as partners and consistently seek to engage them. Summer strategies that experts use include making phone calls, sending e-mails, and mailing postcards to students to welcome them to their classroom (Wild, Mayeaux, and Edmonds 2008). One expert shared how she runs an online book club for students to discuss summer reading prior to them entering her class. Another teacher hosts an ice cream social the week before school starts to allow students to visit the classroom and meet other students.

In the first few days of schools, expert teachers focus on building relationships with and between the students to develop a positive classroom culture. Their classrooms are welcoming, organized, and student friendly, with everything set up for functionality. Experts make students feel instantly welcomed. Students are greeted at the door. Their desks are labeled and ready. The expert engages students in icebreaker-type activities.

One teacher shared how she places a little first-day gift packet on each desk. The first day she takes pictures and posts these in the classroom the next day to make students feel welcome. Another described how students participate in a scavenger hunt in the classroom, so they know where everything is. Everything is designed to engage and create a welcoming climate.

Expert teachers' classrooms are well managed with clear routines and procedures, which are positively communicated and encouraged. Marzano (2008) states that effective teacher practices include clear routines, procedures, and a clear understanding of how these practices contribute to an effective classroom and build trust and respect throughout the class. The classrooms also have organized materials, defined traffic patterns, and use all space such as bulletin boards to further student engagement. Everything in the classroom, from routines to setup, is focused on student success.

Expert Vignette: Building Foundations

Fiona, a high school science teacher, begins nurturing social-emotional attributes from day one. On the first day of class, students are grouped into "family groups" (groups of four) and given an interesting picture. They then brainstorm and generate a list of words connected to their picture. Fiona shares the quote that originally came with the picture. Each quote connects to the social-emotional attributes she wants to bring into focus throughout the course. As students share words, Fiona generates a word list she will use during the warm-ups over the first few weeks to build class culture. Each day, one word will be the focus and students will use these to begin writing goals. Fiona places each student's picture on the goals wall. As the year progresses, the students add notes about their progress toward their goal by their picture. Students are also encouraged to add notes to each other's pictures when they see peers' growth toward their goal. At the end of the course, she takes a new picture and asks students to reflect on how they have grown both academically and interpersonally.

In the first few days and weeks of school, the expert is purposeful in building the foundations of Teacher-Student Kinship and setting a strong classroom culture grounded in strong relationships. Experts focus their efforts on concrete demonstrations of respect for each student and purposefully building trust. Experts build respect through focusing on each individual in the classroom. Experts quickly learn names and something specific about the students. Strategies include surveys about interests, learning history, and how they learn best (Wild, Mayeaux, and Edmonds 2008).

Fiona's unusual start to a high school science class quickly establishes the focus is on growth. This is critical as her students are struggling learners with limited past success in science. Fiona explains that the social-emotional attribute barriers her students brought into her classroom, such as lack of stamina and insecurity about science, had to be resolved if their limited content background knowledge was to be overcome. Her understanding of the need to focus on these skills is why her students succeed more than the teacher who focuses only on content.

Experts build upon respect and begin building trust by establishing and reinforcing high expectations for all students. Experts build trust with and between students by quickly establishing a classroom culture where transparency about errors, needs, and weaknesses is accepted as much as success and strengths are celebrated. The expert focuses on team-building activities where students engage in working together with positive outcomes.

Expert teachers believe social-emotional attributes such as communication skills, initiative, work ethic, and dependability are just as critical to a student's success as content mastery. Experts understand the whole child from their content needs to their learning habit needs to their interpersonal needs. Whereas nonexperts focus primarily on content mastery and possibly learning habits, the experts believe social-emotional attributes are at the heart of a student's success. Experts are able to leverage students' strengths in order to help them learn to reflect on and improve their social-emotional attributes.

This ability is directly connected to the expert's understanding of the whole student. As experts are developing Teacher-Student Kinship, they are building their understanding about the students' strengths and weaknesses in social-emotional attributes. Experts engage students in early reflection and analysis of their own strengths and weaknesses across content, learning habits, and social-emotional attributes. Their focus on understanding the whole student rather than simply understanding that content is the beginning of creating an optimal classroom climate where transparency and support for all students is the norm. Experts teach students to know themselves and to overcome any issues limiting their success.

Experts also work to engage families. Experts send home positive notes the first few weeks about each student. Experts call home with positive messages. Experts find ways for families to positively engage with the learning process from nights designed to highlight students to student-led portfolio show-offs (Wild, Mayeaux, and Edmonds 2003). Experts believe all families are important and focus on helping them in supporting the student.

Expert Vignette: Developing Relationships Every Day

Abby, a middle school teacher, demonstrates that building relationships is a daily process that requires full engagement of the expert and the students. The process also focuses on high expectations and the common language of learning.

> I made a commitment with myself a long time ago to connect with every student who came in my room through what I said a touch noticing them and part of that's because I don't like it when there's invisible children. And I think some children are invisible because it hides their . . . they don't have to work. Nan has a history of being invisible and . . . and sometimes they feel like they're not worthy. They are introverts or whatever the case might be. Anna doesn't talk to me. Anna doesn't talk at all. And . . . and I can say is hello, how are you?
>
> And she'll say, "Fine" and that's all . . . nothing back and forth. So it's easy for me to ignore Anna, but I don't want to ignore Anna. So as we're doing stuff, I'm looking to see who's here and who's not. Seeing, you know, affirming them and there's . . . there's Nickie who's new and she's like so beautiful with her hair. I can see her and I want to make eye contact and acknowledge that we're in this lesson together.

Experts create a classroom culture where everyone is responsible and supportive of each other. Abby is determined to ensure everyone learns to track their learning. She begins class by sharing the expectations for the day and engaging students in a current progress check of each individual student through peer-checks of their agenda. Every Monday, students work together to start the week off with everyone understanding the expectations.

> Here's our class. We have 76.6 percent average. Your agenda needs to be out. I want to make sure you guys write it down every Monday. This will come around. Check to see if the person next to you has their agenda out. If they don't, say Sweetie Pie. If they have it, make sure they are open to page R2. Here it comes. Make sure they write it down.

While students check each other's agendas, she walks around the room to chat with students about different assignments or check on issues they may have had. After a few minutes, she focuses the students on the target of the week, which is beginning a writing assignment due at the end of the week. To introduce the assignment, Abby gives each student a copy of an exemplar piece of writing, similar to the assignment. She then has students analyze the piece for what makes it exemplary. As students work together in pairs, Abby walks around the room questioning their thinking and pushing them to think at a deeper level.

After about ten minutes, students share out a list of their findings. Abby then discusses what will constitute an exemplar for the upcoming assignment using their list. She will use this list for the next few days. By having students define exemplary and create the language for the exemplar, Abby has not only impacted their development of content but also established a common language, thus strengthening their relationships between each other and Abby. The students have also set the expectation.

The expert teacher consistently uses language that promotes learning and instruction (Hattie 2003) to build a strong culture of learning. The language is direct, focused on the instruction, and individualized. Good and Brophy (2008) posit that expert teachers set high and clear expectations for their students. Experts also engage students in the process.

Expert Vignette: Difficult Days

In the midst of a tragic loss of a student, Austin realized the students in his class would not be able to fully engage in learning until they had an opportunity to process the death of their peer. Using an idea, he had read about in a magazine, he created a lesson to help them work through their grief. When students entered the classroom, they found a piece of paper on their desk, which were arranged in a circle. He asked them to write their name on the top of it. Then students passed the paper to their classmate on their right, who was asked to write something they liked about the student. The process continued until every student had written on every piece of paper.

When students received their paper, Austin asked them to read the messages. He then asked them to share what compliment surprised them the most and then what compliment was the most special to them. As the class began to share, the students were moved to tears and sometimes to laughter. After they finished, Austin had them write down things they liked and would miss about their friend. The class then used the list to compose letters to the student's family about their sadness. Finally, the class developed a set of actions they could use to honor the memory of their friend each day as they served and worked together. Austin ended class by thanking students for working together, but then focused them back on the learning goals of the week.

Experts understand that relationships greatly impact learning. When rare tragedy occurs, content learning may need to be pushed back to deal with the social and emotional needs of the students. Ignoring tragedy builds tension. Allowing students to simply process without a structure can lead to chaos. Experts positively build relationships by focusing on students' needs, while returning the focus to the learning.

Expert Vignette: Continuing the Relationships

Expert teachers build Teacher-Student Kinship with students, in order to help students recognize and achieve their potential. Experts believe this relationship is forever. During one of the case study visits for the initial research, Amanda had the privilege of living with an expert for a week. On a trip to the grocery store, the cashier recognized the teacher and ran around the register to hug her.

The expert asked all about the student and the student's sister, whom she had also taught. The student said, "My sister and I are trying to get our college applications done. We thought about calling you to see if you would help us. Is that something you would do?" The teacher quickly agreed. The former student responded, "I knew it! You will always be our teacher."

Experts continue to be supportive of their students, even after the student leaves the expert's class. The knowledge that the expert is forever the student's teacher is highly impactful on the ongoing development of Teacher-Student Kinship.

Expert Vignette: Lifelong Impact

Teacher-Student Kinship is life changing for students. A letter shared by a former student to an expert teacher ten years after the teacher taught the student better describes the impact of the Teacher-Student Kinship relationship.

> Today I went to a training session for a mentoring program that sets up adults with students in grades three to twelve. We were each asked about someone who has been a great mentor in our lives and I shared about my spectacular seventh and eighth grade math teacher who made me realize that math wasn't the devil after all (just word problems). Afterwards, I realized I had never shared with you how much you impacted my life. I hope this helps you to know just how wonderful and invaluable your presence in my life has been.
>
> Before I got to your school, I really struggled both in school and out of it, because of bullying. I had become very withdrawn and my teachers in elementary school thought I might be a special needs student, because I had no confidence socially or academically. At a new school, I really hoped things would be different. I dove straight into your school where most of the students had known each other since elementary school or before.
>
> After a few weeks, it didn't seem like I was really going to fit in anywhere, and although the bullying improved, it didn't go away entirely. But one thing did change and it was that you took an active interest in me. Our shared experience of moving around a lot allowed me to connect to a teacher for the first time in years. More than that, you taught me that not only was math not inherently evil, but that I could actually do well and even enjoy it. I started to build confidence little by little, and even when I was teased by other students for not being in the talented and gifted class, it started to matter less and less.
>
> Slowly, I started to realize I could not only solve math problems, but the problems that had been plaguing me for years. I began to stand up to my bullies and put an end to it. I might not be able to stop every rumor and I might not

have many friends, but I was happy and I wasn't going to let anyone else try to take that away. I still remember placing in that math tournament and being so proud to have been part of it, especially since we were the only public school to place that year.

To this day, I still like algebra (although I despise trig) and I feel capable of tackling whatever challenges come my way, whether social or academic. Honestly I don't know where I would be without your support during those two difficult years. Of all the teachers I have ever had, you truly have had the most significant impact on the course of my life. Each and every one of your students is blessed to be a part of your class. I look forward to sharing some of the lessons I learned from you as I move forward and try to provide a positive influence on the next generation.

NOTE OF CAUTION

With everything in life, there are positives and negatives. The negative side of the Teacher-Student Kinship relationship is when the rare event occurs where a student drastically fails or is lost and the expert perceives it as a personal failure. Expert teachers, like experts in most domains, show more emotionality about successes and failures in their work. Berliner (2004) claimed experts' sense of responsibility played a part in their feelings about their work. Through the research, expert teachers shared their deeply personal commitment to students, but they also shared occasional overwhelming feelings of responsibility.

Experts often will take on tough situations, tough classes, and difficult students. Their successes, which are exponential, have little impact on their emotions, because the results align with what they expected to happen due to their expertise. Failure is defined as not meeting the standards they set for themselves and for their students. Failure is never considered and therefore completely unexpected. When it happens, failure impacts the expert teacher very deeply.

In the discussions with expert teachers, they were asked to describe a problem in their classroom they failed to overcome. Interestingly, not one expert could describe such a situation. The question was reworded to ask about a situation they considered a failure. Every single expert emotionally described something outside of their classroom and expressed tremendous regret over the various situations. These incidents profoundly impacted the expert and their trust in peers and leadership.

Outside of school issues negatively impacting the student was the most mentioned issue by experts. These issues ranged from abuse of students to illegal activity to homelessness. In each case, the expert reached out to school officials and community resources without success. One teacher described how she had been counseled by her administration for overstepping her boundaries in trying to help a family find a home in the school district after being evicted. The family was evicted and the student dropped out. The student was killed. The teacher was so devastated that she spiraled into depression. She sought counseling and transferred a few years later to a different school.

Each of these situations illustrates elements of caution concerning expert teachers. Due to their extreme feelings of responsibility toward the students, they will go to great lengths to help their students. If these actions fail, extreme emotions and consequences may follow. Section III further discusses the needs and supports expert teachers require from leadership and peers to thrive and succeed.

POINTS TO PONDER

- Teacher-Student Kinship is the nucleus to all the decisions, choices, and actions an expert makes.
- Expert teachers purposefully develop and continually refine Teacher-Student Kinship with students in order to gain Whole Student Understanding.
- Expert teachers seek to have a lifelong impact upon their students.
- When students are not the center of other professionals' motivation and focus, experts struggle to trust and respect these peers.

Section II

THE THINKING PROCESSES OF EXPERT TEACHERS

Every education major completes preservice coursework in learning theories and educational psychology. Various theories are held at different levels of effectiveness based much on the preference of the instructor teaching the course. The truth is learning about the student and the needs of the student. Experts do not prefer one type of learning over the other. Rather, experts are well versed in various theories of learning and are able to employ the most appropriate in their classrooms based upon their Whole Student Understanding.

Teacher-Student Kinship is the nucleus at the center of every choice an expert teacher makes. Their ability to build these dynamic, critical relationships is only part of the expert teacher equation. While Teacher-Student Kinship allows experts to develop a deep Whole Student Understanding about each student, equally important is their use of their Expert Lens to focus on issues and refine these through their Expert Teacher Thinking Process.

The focus of this section is to define the Expert Lens and illustrate how experts use the Expert Teacher Thinking Process to guide and facilitate student development toward Conceptual Mastery. Chapter 4, "The Expert Lens," defines the elements of the Expert Lens and how these elements interact in the choices experts make in the classroom. Chapter 5 describes the expert thinking process or the process experts use to find solutions to both large and small issues.

The development of the Expert Lens to focus and use in the Expert Teacher Thinking process is described in chapters 6–8. Each chapter is designed to give the readers both a conceptual understanding of expert thinking and processing and practical exercises to aid in development toward expertise.

Chapter 6, "Creating Conceptual Mastery," describes the elaborate planning that expert teachers use to create the elements of Conceptual Mastery.

In chapter 7, "Learning Segments," the focus is on how experts develop and use smaller chunks of learning to push students toward Conceptual Mastery. Finally, chapter 8, "The Day-to-Day," is about the day-to-day lessons in the expert's classroom.

SECTION II: THINKING QUESTIONS

- What are the implications when teachers focus on understanding why issues occur, rather than focusing first on how to correct the issues?
- How does the elaborate planning process impact the expert's ability to make choices in the classroom more effectively?
- Why is Whole Student Understanding critical to the development and use of the Expert Lens?

Chapter 4

The Expert Lens

While Teacher-Student Kinship is the motivating nucleus of all choices experts make, the Expert Lens is the tool they use to understand, clarify, analyze, evaluate, and select those choices. Because the experts are extremely motivated by Teacher-Student Kinship, they seek to constantly develop their Expert Lens to better focus on the needs of the whole student. Their entire vision about teaching and learning is through this focus. They consistently analyze students' strengths and weaknesses per the lens to make instructional choices. They also analyze through this lens to understand their own strengths and weaknesses concerning their professional learning needs.

THE EXPERT LENS DEFINED

The Expert Lens is the kaleidoscope lens through which experts view teaching and learning. They apply the lens to every moment in the classroom, but hyper-focus the lens when issues arise to understand the reasons why issues are occurring before deciding on possible solutions.

A nonexpert views teaching and learning in the classroom differently from the expert teacher. The nonexpert sees the daily objectives and the issues associated with these objectives. Their lens is often focused using their strongest skills. If the teacher considers themselves a content master, their lens views all issues as content-related and choices will be made based primarily on their content knowledge. For example, if a child is struggling with multiplication, the teacher will not consider the pedagogical approach to teaching the child multiplication to be the issue.

The nonexpert will then simply give more of the same content reinforcement to the child. When the child fails to master the information, the teacher will simply blame the child. Nonexperts view teaching as a simplistic act. They deliver information, children receive, practice, and master. When this does not work, the nonexperts fall back to their own strength (see figure 4.1).

Another example of the nonexpert is the teacher with highly developed social-emotional attributes but limited content and pedagogical knowledge. These teachers have fun classrooms, where all the children enjoy themselves and engage in fun activities. These children are making cotton-ball cloud models and creating toothpick bridges with fun troll stories, but none of the learning is connected to strong content requirements. These are teachers who everyone expects to have great results but in the end everything was fun fluff.

Expert teachers have highly developed content knowledge, pedagogical knowledge, and interpersonal knowledge. These teachers understand the importance of each type of knowledge and the interdependence required to have success for each student. Experts also have highly developed understandings of how each element works together for the greater good, because they deeply and intrinsically understand each part and its place in teaching and learning.

Expert teachers view teaching and learning in the classroom differently. When expert teachers suspect there is an issue in the classroom, they focus their expert lens through their Whole Child Understanding to gather evidence about the issue. The expert teacher receives the feedback through their expert lens and filters through their hyperdeveloped content knowledge, pedagogical knowledge, and interpersonal knowledge, in a systematic and interconnected manner. Through this focusing and refocusing, experts seek to understand why the issue is happening, before activating solutions on how to correct it (see figure 4.2).

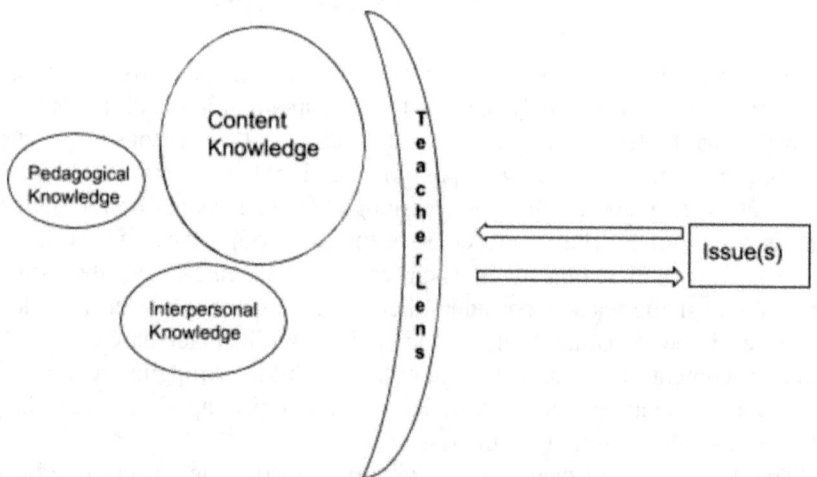

Figure 4.1 The Nonexpert Lens

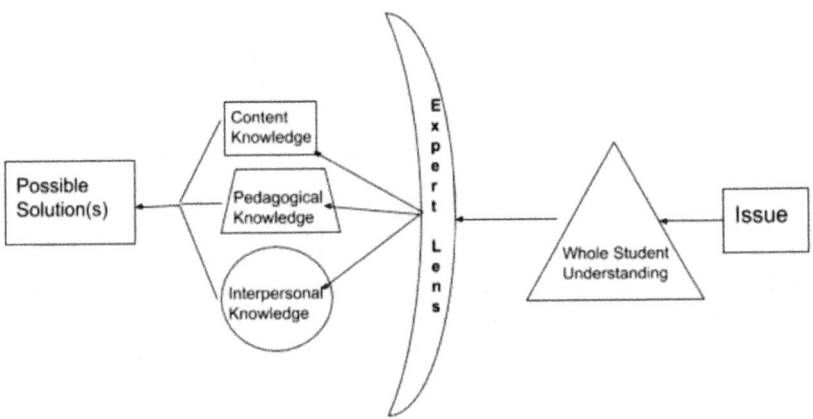

Figure 4.2 The Expert Lens

Each sub-lens is highly developed and is used not only systematically but also intuitively. The foundation, as previously discussed, is their Whole Student Understanding, but their highly developed content, pedagogical, and social-emotional attributes are also the key to their abilities.

Content Lens

In Amanda's second-year teaching, she was teaching middle school mathematics in a small rural school. One of her eighth-grade math students, Mike, was a really smart student but often difficult and abrasive. In the middle of teaching a lesson in chapter 4, which was finding the percentage in a real-world scenario using $x = \% \times y$, Mike raised his hand and said, "You remember how we learned to find x in chapter 2 and I looked to see that we learn how to find y in chapter 5? Well, I think you should have taught it all together and it would have made more sense. You need to help us make the connections. So, why didn't you do that?"

The Content Lens is grounded in standards and expectations of the content. Content is where expert teachers begin, because ultimately, they believe students should have mastered the content. While some would state content mastery is what students must know and be able to do, expert teachers move beyond that to believe their content is only a thread of all learning. Experts have students master their content in such a way that they make connections across the discipline and between other contents to be a truly educated individual.

Hattie (2003) states that experts have deep representations about teaching and learning, and while experts and experienced teachers demonstrate little differences in the amount of content and pedagogical knowledge they have, experts organize and use content knowledge in a more effective and integrated manner. Experts understand the differences between knowledge, skills, and processes needed to achieve conceptual content mastery of their subject. A simple example would be to consider mathematics broadly as a discipline. In mathematics, some foundation knowledge, often referred to as number sense, is required, in which students conceptually understand the number system and can apply this understanding fluently to solve basic problems.

Upon this foundational understanding is built conceptual content understanding of the various branches of mathematics, from algebra to trigonometry to calculus. The final layer is the students' ability to make connections across the branches using their foundational skills fluently to solve complex problems, create new problems, and communicate their understanding with precision and elegance. The mastery of mathematics is recursive and ever-developing and the expert understands this infinite process.

The expert also understands their course is only a piece in the process. The experts exhibit deep understanding about the expectations of prior grade levels and upcoming grade levels. This vertical understanding is a hinge upon many of the choices concerning the day-to-day learning. The expert also has a deep understanding of how the content connects to other contents and uses those connections to grow students. Basically, experts are better at making connections, because their content knowledge is wide and deep. What Mike taught Amanda was to look past the units as to see the whole picture, and then use that understanding to create conceptual understandings for students.

When choosing how to teach the content to students, the expert is able to access their vast knowledge of learning theories to choose the most effective combination of theories for any given lesson. For example, at the introduction of a unit, the expert may allow students to work collaboratively to brainstorm, make connections, and construct their knowledge within a social context. However, in the midst of learning a process, the expert may use direct instruction to clearly model for students the steps in a process.

Experts do not have a standard one-size-fits-all type of lesson but rather teach based on the requirements of the content and the needs of the whole student. This ability to choose the best lesson structure on any given day begins with their elaborate planning process and continues through their constant reflection of their students' learning.

Pedagogical Lens: Teaching and Learning

The Pedagogical Lens is what is often considered the "Teacher Toolbox" and is built from the strategies and structures teachers and students use to teach and learn together. These pedagogical methods maximize the teaching and learning to achieve learning. The expert teachers' highly developed pedagogical knowledge engages all forms of teaching and learning. Their ability to choose specific methods and strategies for each student hinges on their highly developed Content and Interpersonal Knowledge. The strategies are focused on building classroom culture, as well as meeting individual student learning needs.

Expert teachers maximize their choices to build students' learning habits. They initiate the process by helping students to understand their own learning needs, and then work throughout the year to develop students' independence by developing their learning habits. Experts know when to use concrete strategies and when to move students past these concrete strategies to think abstractly. Experts also know when the whole class needs a strategy and when small groups or individuals need a strategy. Experts do not force all students to use strategies they do not need. For to do so would stunt their move toward independence.

Interpersonal Lens: Knowledge of Students

The Interpersonal Lens is the lens focused most on relationship-building between teacher and students, between the students, and in building self-reflection in the student. The difference is that the expert builds these relationships as part of the learning rather than isolated relationship-building tasks. They begin the year by delving deeply in the process of knowing their students, academically, socially, and emotionally. Their carefully crafted lessons are tailored to the needs and interests of their students and to build students' interpersonal attributes. These lessons are the backbone of their powerfully positive classroom culture. Rather than seeing content and pedagogy as something separate from culture, experts use the content and their lessons to build culture.

The attributes of students such as perseverance, stamina, open-mindedness, equity, trust, and self-reflection are critical not only to the class culture but also to the individual student's success. Experts understand how creating a classroom culture where errors are welcome and discussion flows freely connects to the overall success of the whole student. Experts are daily reflectors of their practice because they know attributes such as perseverance and self-regulation are developed one day at a time over a year of learning.

Expert teachers are highly engaged with students and with their work. Hattie (2003, 8) states, "The manner used by the teacher to treat the students, respect them as learners and people, and demonstrate care and commitment for them are attributes of expert teachers." By having such respect coupled with their content understanding, they can recognize possible barriers to learning and can seek ways to overcome these barriers by developing interpersonal attributes and learning habits. The picture drawn of experts is one of involvement and caring for the students, a willingness to be receptive to what the students need, not attempting to dominate the situation.

DEVELOPING THE EXPERT LENS

The Expert Lens is developed over time as the expertise of the teacher is developed. However, experts are constantly readjusting and refining their lens to have a sharper focus on their students and maximize the Teacher-Student Kinship. Three professional practices are critical to this constant sharpening of the focus: (1) elaborate planning, (2) gathering evidence of student learning, and (3) professional learning.

The overarching goal they set for their students is for each to achieve Conceptual Mastery, where students have a strong conceptual understanding of content, can maximize learning habits, and apply strong social-emotional attributes. These goals are strongly interconnected and interdependent. For example, expert teachers understand the conceptual mastery of a content is not possible if students do not have possess and use learning habits.

This complex understanding of the interplay among the three elements is why the way the expert thinks, plans, and implements instruction is different. Rather than simply marching students toward a specific, quick goal, experts create a rich, interconnected, purposefully designed experience each day for each student in order to help all reach the powerful Conceptual Mastery. Their Expert Lens is always focused to this end.

The Expert Lens is dependent on the elaborate planning expert teachers use to design and implement the learning. The experts' ability to create dynamic, rigorous, student-centered lessons originally begins in their elaborate analyzing and processing of the content in view of the students' needs. While some teachers plan to have a plan, experts plan to understand, process, create, and implement dynamic lessons for their specific students.

Expert teachers plan and process their content with the goal of engaging students in rigorous learning that will impact the whole child, not just academic expectations. While many teachers simply pull the given curriculum, read the lesson plans day by day, expert teachers delve deeply into their content to analyze and evaluate standards, curriculum, assessments, suggested materials, and choose additional pieces.

Their complex understanding of their content (Hattie 2003) is consistently evidenced in their elaborate planning. While expert teachers have different structures they may use to plan, an elaborate three-phase planning process was found through the study. The process resembles the powerful Understanding by Design model (Wiggins and McTighe 2011) but is more conceptually focused on the whole child meeting Conceptual Mastery.

Expert teachers plan the year as a whole with the Whole Student Understanding in focus, then move to Short-Term Goal planning, and then to the daily lessons. They have an exact vision of where each student will be at the end of the year from the very first day of school. This learning continuum vision is both for the class as a whole and for each student and is beyond what most would consider realistic expectations.

Their elaborate planning is critical in several ways. First and foremost, their content knowledge is constantly deepening through this process. Second, because expert teachers have planned the year as a whole, they deeply understand how each unit and each day fits into the whole scheme of the year. Third, experts understand all of the connections across the year. Therefore, experts are able to pre-assess students' strengths and weaknesses and make adjustments; they are able to highlight skills and information at critical junctures and then ensure students master these elements prior to the needed application. Finally, they also have time to build skills, strategies, and practices as needed, because they know how each piece fits together well in advance of the need for mastery.

Plans are fluid, while expectations are solid. Modifications to the plans occur based on the needs of the students and the daily reflection of the teacher, but the focus on the overarching goals does not change.

The elaborate planning process of expert teachers runs counter to current models of scripted lessons and top-down development curricula. The expert teacher embraces standards but is beyond the lock-in-step curricula often used to "teacher-proof" education. The experts' deep understanding of the content has been sharpened through their constant working through the standards and consistent reflection on how students learn and grow. When districts and states circumvent and try to standardize this arduous process, the development of expertise is hindered.

The Expert Lens is further sharpened through the daily, almost moment by moment, reflection and refinement. Experts are able to analyze issues and improvise during a lesson very quickly due to their expertise, but they also spend great amounts of time reflecting and refining their craft based on their current context of students.

The expert teacher's weakness is the inability to generalize. They are extremely context bound to their current students and their needs, which is directly connected to their strong Teacher-Student Kinship. These teachers are not searching Pinterest for a quick, fun activity. They are processing classroom issues at an extremely complex level and working through all sorts of solutions to find the best strategies for their current students. If a strategy works consistently for many students, it may become a classroom standard, but the expert will refine it with each use to specifically fit the needs of the students.

Finally, the focus of the Expert Lens is sharpened through professional learning. Expert teachers make choices about professional learning based on the specific needs they see in their teaching, their perceived weaknesses in their own craft, solely to improve their students' academic achievement. Deep-impact professional learning, such as National Board certification, is highly motivating to the expert, as these meet the needs of the expert.

SEEING THROUGH THE EXPERT LENS

The Expert Lens is always focused on gathering evidence about students and their learning. The expert teacher's Expert Lens is hyper-focused on the actions and reactions, words, body language, facial expressions, discussions, work of the students throughout the learning process. The expert teacher also understands that everything in the classroom is evidence. The next chapter explains how the expert uses their Expert Lens in the Expert Teacher Thinking Process and the next three chapters in the section focus how the Expert Lens is developed and used in the classroom.

NOTE OF CAUTION

The Expert Lens is developed through rigorous reflection and constant refinement. The expert develops this lens in response to the deep Teacher-Student Kinship they have with their students. When reform efforts push down "teacher-proof" quick solutions, such as scripted lessons and lock-step curricula, the opportunities to develop the Expert Lens in teachers are limited. Over fifty years of reform efforts aimed at building more standardized lesson and assessments have yielded little results. If reform efforts for the next fifty years focus on developing experts in every classroom, success for all students will be possible.

POINTS TO PONDER

- *Content Expertise* is more than simply being proficient in content knowledge, but rather having a deeply developed conceptual framework of content and all the ways the content connects across disciplines and integrates metacognition.

- *Learning Habits* are continually developed and refined in the expert's classroom. Experts understanding teaching a student to learn is equally as critical as teaching them the content.
- *Social-Emotional Attributes* are the fine threads connecting students to others and to themselves. Helping students to refine these by building on their strengths and reflecting on ways to improve their weaknesses is critical to their present and future success.

Chapter 5

The Expert Teacher Thinking Processes

Expert teachers think and process differently from nonexpert teachers. First, they view themselves as fellow learners in the classroom. Experts believe students are in the class to master content, but they also believe they are there to teach lifelong learning skills and social-emotional attributes. Additionally, experts are always seeking evidence to learn about the students and about their own teaching. Everyone is a learner. This perspective creates a very different learning process in expert teachers' classroom, which is part of the reason why their students are more successful in all aspects of mastery.

The process is recursive, highly reflective, and engages all learners in real-time discussions. While not linear, for ease of understanding, the process is conceptualized by understanding how the basic elements work together. The basic elements are to finding why and then finding what the solutions are: Collect Evidence, Analyze Evidence, Develop Solutions, Implement Solutions, Refine Solutions, and Norm Solutions (see figure 5.1).

In all aspects of teaching and learning, the expert teacher uses Expert Teacher Thinking process. The process is used to make choices about teaching and learning and to solve issues that may arise during the teaching and learning. The Expert Teacher Thinking process is not linear but rather recursive and constantly evolving due to new feedback from, between, and among the students. Learners are humans. Our thinking evolves daily and is impacted by internal and external forces. Expert teachers understand the daily recursive nature of the learning process and are constantly gathering evidence, analyzing the evidence, developing strategies to overcome issues, refining the strategies to meet individual needs, and then finally norming the strategies so students use them intuitively to learn. Additionally, expert teachers do not take on process alone but teach and engage their students in this recursive, reflective process.

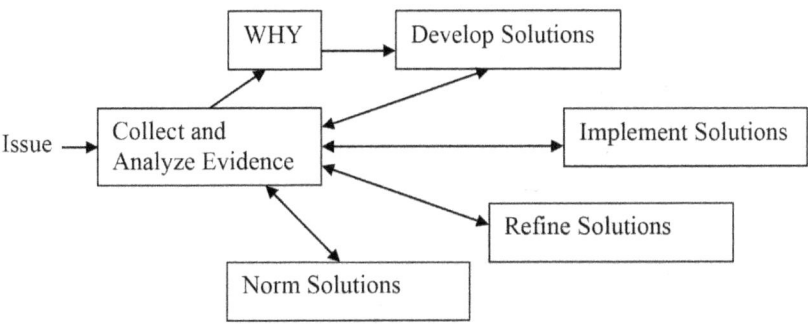

Figure 5.1   The Expert Teacher Thinking Process

EVIDENCE VERSUS DATA

Over the past two decades, the term "data-driven decision making" has been one of the trendy buzzwords in education. This term supports the massive push for annual standardized testing, which has given way to districts and schools embracing a year-long program of shorter standardized assessments for teachers and school leaders to track student progress. While the process would appear to be aligned with expert thinking, the issue is what schools track is simple data. Data answer the basic "what" question in a very simple number format. Data only reveal where a child is in their academic learning at a given point. Data can be, when used appropriately, an entry point into further exploration. Data do not explain why and will not lead to an effective how.

Experts rely on complex evidence in addition to simple data. Evidence tells the expert why something is happening, so the how the expert chooses can then align to the need. Evidence is everything from student work to observations of students. An expert teacher's ability to anticipate, plan, and improvise in given situations is critical to student success and based upon the evidence the expert is constantly gathering, analyzing, and evaluating. Experts are more adaptable at anticipating problems and then improvising, because they focus more of their solution time gaining an understanding of the problem by monitoring ongoing solution attempts, constantly and consistently checking for accuracy, and updating or elaborating problem representations as new constraints emerge (Hattie 2003; Voss and Post 1988).

EXPERT TEACHER FEEDBACK

In the expert teacher's classroom, feedback is a purposeful two-way communication between all learners in the classroom that is used as evidence to make next step decisions. Expert teachers crave, use, and perpetuate this feedback for very purposeful reasons. First, experts crave evidence to understand what students know and do not know. This heightened, consistent, and constant evidence-gathering is one of the triggers to all learners experiencing Flow in the classroom. Hattie (2012) clearly defines the importance of feedback and how teachers and students use such feedback to achieve results. In the expert teacher's classroom, feedback is everything and everything is feedback. Unlike the nonexpert, feedback is not about the grade or about the right answer. Feedback is ongoing evidence about why something is happening, so the expert can make connections to understand the root cause of the issue.

Experts are highly engaged with students and the learning processes, because of their Teacher-Student Kinship; therefore, they experience Flow from the engagement and interactions.

As one teacher described it,

When everything is just popping, you know it. You have the extremely sharpened sense of every action and reaction in the classroom and you are able to respond with a sort of automaticity. My favorite is when all of the students are in the zone with me and are just moving as one learning unit. It is an incredible feeling. (Chandra, elementary school)

Expert Teacher Feedback is also different from other teachers' use of feedback in terms of purpose. Expert teachers seek evidence from students to understand where they are in the learning continuum and to understand why about all the elements in that continuum. Expert teachers give and receive consistent feedback focused on the work of the students to make decisions about next steps. Feedback is often viewed as the information a teacher uses to give a student grade about an assignment, but expert feedback is about evidence, which is much more complex and critical. Experts go beyond the use of feedback effective teachers use to make deeper connections. Expert teachers use feedback to guide instruction and to engage students in understanding what the students know, what the students do not know, and what the students still needs to learn.

Experts perpetuate feedback in three main frames, which are distinct and interconnected: *Nimble Feedback*, which is the agile, on-the-spot, day-to-day feedback; *Targeted Feedback*, which is focused on moving students toward mastering short-term chunks; and *Persistent Feedback*, which is an holistic feedback focused on helping students persist toward conceptual mastery. In the following vignette, Expert Teacher Thinking Process and the use of feedback are illustrated.

Expert Vignette: Teacher Talk

The statewide assessment for Algebra I was a few weeks away and all of the Algebra I teachers decided to give the students a thorough review of the material. Surprisingly to some of the teachers, the Algebra I students in all the classes, except for Mrs. Jones's classes, were consistently struggling to solve linear function problems. The unit had been the first one of the year, so the teachers were frustrated with this emerging problem.

During their weekly meeting Mrs. Grey quipped, "Well, I taught it to them. They don't remember a thing I say. I am just going to drill them again tomorrow."

Mr. Besser stated, "They just aren't motivated to think. I have to spoon-feed them everything. I guess I can get out that practice workbook and make them do some more pages."

Finally, Mrs. Jones asked, "Well, are there any common mistakes? Do they have a common misunderstanding?"

"What do you mean?" asked Mrs. Jarred, "We all know you have the smart ones."

Ignoring the untrue little jab, Mrs. Jones continued, "I am simply asking if we know why they are struggling, before we worry about what to do and how to fix it."

Flustered, most of the teachers ignored her question and began blaming the lazy, unmotivated students in their classrooms.

The initial discussion of the teachers is indicative of what is considered teaching in many schools. On a daily basis in classrooms across the nation, lessons happen in an ineffective process. Teachers talk. Students listen. Teachers assume. Students misunderstand. Students do work. Teachers may or may not check the work. Teachers give a grade. Teachers blame students for failing. Teachers give more work. Students fail again. Teachers decide students are hopeless. Students give up. The process repeats itself.

As found in the discussion, teachers often place all of the responsibility of learning on the students. The teachers' low self-efficacy concerning their impact on the students' mastery of content prevents them from understanding they have the power to change the process. When students misunderstand or fail, the teacher simply adds more of the same work, assuming more practice will correct the problem. This thinking is equivalent to giving a person cough syrup for pink eye and wondering why the eye is not clearing up. In teaching, little importance is placed in teaching teachers to diagnose the causes of issues, make instructional choices, and engage the students in the process. Rather teachers and schools seek quick fixes and ineffective remedies. When these do not work, the students are obviously "lazy," "unmotivated," or "unable to think."

Expert Vignette: Collecting Evidence

After the meeting, Mrs. Chin, a first-year teacher, stopped by Mrs. Jones's class to ask her, "I am not sure what you meant by your questions, but I would really appreciate any help you could give me."

Since her planning period was next, Mrs. Jones offered to go to Mrs. Chin's class the next hour and work with the students.

The class began with students working silently on a worksheet, but Mrs. Jones quickly stopped the students and told them, "We are going to try something out. Mrs. Chin said you were hardworking students, who could help me with an experiment on partner talk. What I want you to do is sit in pairs. Now, Partner A is going to work all of the odd problems and Partner B is going to work all of the even problems, but one at a time. However, when you are working your problem, I want you to talk out what you are doing and why. The partner, who is not working, will listen, and record your thinking on their worksheets. Simple! Mrs. Chin and I will be walking around and asking some questions."

Mrs. Chin whispered, "It kind of makes me nervous when they talk."

Mrs. Jones replied, "How do you know what they are thinking, if they don't talk?"

For the next ten minutes, the pair of teachers walked around the classroom, listening, and asking questions. Mrs. Jones motioned Mrs. Chin to come over to listen to one pair discussing a problem.

"I always get the hard questions," said Jaquan, "You know the ones where the table is not easy to figure out."

"Why do you think your question is hard?" asked Mrs. Jones.

"Well, you see the last problem, Beth did? The table grew by two, so it was easy. Mine is not growing, but getting smaller, and not by the same number! So how can I find the slope? I don't even understand."

"Do you have another method for finding slope?" asked Mrs. Jones.

"I don't know," said Jaquan, "I just don't get this stupid stuff."

Mrs. Chin began to explain Jaquan was not an easy student, but Mrs. Jones raised her hand and stopped her.

"Let's talk about this after school, but if you are ok with me working with them for a few moments. I think I can clear up some misunderstandings."

Whereas nonexperts seek feedback to give a grade or quell a problem, expert teachers are extremely adept at understanding what needs quick attention and what can take time to develop. Mrs. Jones's mastery of using feedback to understand, analyze, and evaluate learner needs to make important decisions is evidence of her expertise. More importantly, she engaged and integrated all learners in giving and receiving feedback through the learning to understand their thinking.

In the day-to-day learning cycle, the expert teacher focuses the Expert Lens primarily through Nimble Feedback. Nimble Feedback is quick, light, and agile feedback the learners use to facilitate and guide the learning in the classroom in real time, as Mrs. Jones did when interacting with the students.

The expert is constantly listening, asking questions, recording patterns, and focusing on finding the root of any issue. Nimble feedback is students' quick response to a partner's question about the learning or the questions they ask in a discussion. Of all the feedback used, Nimble Feedback is the most powerful, because Nimble Feedback allows the learners to catch misconceptions before these take root. Nimble Feedback seems almost effortless but is based on the total immersion in the learning happening in the classroom. Expert teachers are constantly scanning, analyzing, evaluating, and adjusting the learning based on the feedback they are receiving from the students. Additionally, the students in the classroom engage in the Nimble Feedback through their responses and engagement with the teacher and with their peers. Nimble Feedback is more than simple "with-it-ness," because the expert is seeking to find the reasons why things are happening to make critical judgments and adjustments. From the outside, the class seems to simply flow smoothly, but under the surface, hundreds of quick decisions and adjustments are occurring, all due to Nimble Feedback occurring among all of the learners.

Nimble Feedback is the key to maintaining an engaged and positive learning environment. Nimble Feedback allows learners to engage with each other and to experience true culture, because everyone is responsible for everyone, every minute of every day. Nimble Feedback is also the secret to a culture where students feel safe to fail and safe to succeed.

Expert Vignette: Developing Solutions

> Mrs. Jones found the *why* behind the misconceptions through her purposeful questions and observations of the students. She used a content-related question when she asked Jaquan about why he thought his question was hard. She sought the why of the pedagogical issues by observing the students as they worked the problems to understand how Mrs. Chin had taught the material. She also purposefully engaged with Jaquan to understanding the why of his reactions. While this was happening, Mrs. Jones was mentally analyzing and evaluating all of these pieces to develop a solution.

When expert teachers encounter issues, they always seek to understand first and foremost why something is happening, before they begin considering how to fix the issue. Much like a doctor diagnosing a condition before offering solutions, experts understanding the reason why something is or is not happening is critical to choosing the right solution. The why may be a content-related issue, a pedagogical issue, or an interpersonal issue. Often the issue is a combination. Making choices and solving problems must begin with the why as the first step. If the underlying issue is not properly diagnosed, the how that follows will be ineffective.

The Expert Teacher Thinking Process is effective because expert teachers have built strong relationships in their classrooms through Teacher-Student Kinship. Second, expert teachers have a highly developed Expert Lens, which means their content knowledge, pedagogical knowledge, and interpersonal knowledge are all functioning simultaneously and intuitively at expert levels. Finally, experts plan deeply with a laser focus on the expectations and their students' needs. These three elements support their ability to recognize issues early, analyze, and engage students in solutions before the issue becomes insurmountable.

At the beginning of the chapter, the other teachers were quick to blame the students. The lens they view issues through is one that shows the students' effort or lack thereof is the cause, so more practice must be the solution. They focus on the students' actions rather than on their own actions, due in part to their low self-efficacy and poorly developed content and pedagogical skills. The nonexpert sees learning as linear. The content is taught, students practice, the test is given, and a grade is assigned (see figure 5.2).

The expert teacher sees the learning as a recursive continuum of complexly woven pieces including content, learning habits, and social-emotional attributes. They also understand that the learning is maximized through recursive interactions in the classroom and through helping students to build strategies to aid in developing their learning habits. The expert does not see a misconception or mistake as a negative but rather simply as evidence of where the student is in the process. This evidence is used to better understand why the student has the misconception. This information will then help both the teacher and the student choose strategies to help the student progress toward mastery. Additionally, the expert understands the interconnectivity of each piece of the content and how it weaves together toward conceptual mastery.

The evidence alerts the expert teacher (and sometimes the student) that an issue has arisen. This is the moment when experts shine. Rather than jumping to a cookie-cutter solution, experts focus their Expert Lens and begin to seek understanding and clarity by asking why. Seeking the why is context-bound in the specific issue. Experts ask questions, observe students work, listen to their conversations, and clarify the issues.

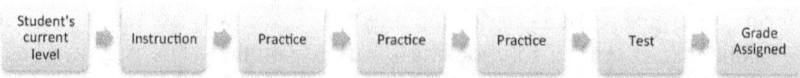

Figure 5.2 Nonexpert Thinking Process

Expert Vignette: Implementing Solutions

Mrs. Jones proceeded to the board where she drew a graph, a table, an equation, and a set of points. She then began to help the class make connections between the ways a linear function problem could be presented. She then had everyone share how they found slope, which was by using the numbers in the table. The issue was when the slope was a fraction or if they had no table, the students struggled. Mrs. Jones reminded them of the slope formula. She then taught them how to think through such problems using a set of specific thinking questions. Mrs. Jones then had the students pair up again and work the rest of the problems using the thinking questions, while she and Mrs. Chin observed. Mrs. Jones made a point to reaffirm Jaquan's effort in using the thinking questions to solve the problems and support his partner. By the end of the class, all of the students were more confident. Mrs. Jones gave each student a set of four problems as an exit ticket. Jaquan gave Mrs. Chin a high five on the way out the door. After school, the two teachers met to discuss the results.

Mrs. Jones's deep understanding of content led her to know Mrs. Chin had taught the concept in a very simplified manner and the students did not have a conceptual understanding of how the problems were connected. Thus, they struggled to make complex connections to more difficult problems. Her pedagogical knowledge helped her deconstruct how Mrs. Chin had taught the content and why the students were simply repeating what they had been taught. The secret here is students really do what they are taught. Her interpersonal knowledge of students helped her to understand the why behind Jaquan's behavior and be compassionate.

Expert Vignette: Refining Solutions

After evaluating the exit tickets and finding the class had improved tremendously, Mrs. Chin said, "This is amazing. . . . It's like magic. Even Jaquan has all of the answers right and was smiling when he left. He never smiles. I just don't understand. How did you just walk into my room and see the issue . . . fix the issue. I don't understand."

Mrs. Jones smiled, "Because I always ask 'why' before worrying about how. Let me outline the whys. First, why were they struggling with slope? Well, you taught your students to find slope by finding the difference between the y values on a table. Correct? This simple method works if the y values are positive, consecutive whole numbers, and if they have a table. The state assessment problems you gave them had much more complicated situations, so they were clueless. Your teaching did not match what the students had to know and be able to do. Secondly, why were they not able to make connections across different types of problems? Well, you have never modeled that thinking for them using specific thinking questions to model how to think through the problems based on the given information. So, I gave them a few thinking questions and modeled it for them. They practiced these questions rather than just rote working problems and they became more independent problem solvers. Now no matter what type of linear function problem they have, they can find the entry point, make connections, and solve. Finally, why was Jaquan suddenly so rude? You see, Jaquan is not 'bad,' but he was frustrated after he tried and failed. He has little perseverance. He is used to quick success or quitting. Instead of saying he is confused, he lashed out due to his insecurity and uncertainty. He wants to save face and he doesn't feel safe in saying he is struggling. I simply helped him be successful, so he would engage. Then I reinforced his efforts."

Mrs. Chin said, "I think I have a few things to learn. I never thought about considering why kids are doing something or not understanding something, or even acting out."

Mrs. Jones smiled, "We all have much to learn. Teaching is tough. If you aren't eager to learn, you aren't eager to teach. I suggest you begin by learning to listen to students, gather evidence, and ask why, before you add extra work."

After processing the complexities of the why of the situation, Mrs. Jones began to efficiently develop and test solutions in real time. Mrs. Jones's knowledge of how to correct the issue was grounded in her highly developed Expert Lens. Using her content knowledge, she built off of what they had learned from Mrs. Chin but helped them make purposeful connections. Pedagogically, she modeled her thinking and gave the students thinking questions to apply. She also used graphic representations to help students make connections between the different types of problems. Finally, she applied her deep understanding of social-emotional attributes to help students feel success, encourage them to persistent, and praise their efforts. Critical to the success found in this example is how Mrs. Jones used her Expert Lens to understand why students had misconceptions, before she tried solutions.

At the end of the day, Mrs. Jones and Mrs. Chin sat together and evaluated the impact of the effort. Mrs. Jones's solution pieces were successful, as demonstrated by the exit tickets and Jaquan's reaction at the end of the class. However, this was simply one day and one issue. If Mrs. Chin is to become an expert teacher, Mrs. Jones will have to help her repeat this process over and over until it becomes intuitive as it is in Mrs. Jones's class. Additionally, Mrs. Jones will have to mentor Mrs. Chin's understanding of how to not only develop and implement solutions but also reinforce and refine the solutions until these become part of the students' normal practice.

Mrs. Jones did not walk into her first year of teaching understanding how to teach students to deeply and conceptually understand linear functions. She built her unit from years of asking why. She then had thinking questions and visuals; she knew would work for any student.

Mrs. Jones also examined what had been taught, before she focused on students' efforts. Expert teachers focus on the impact of their teaching when seeking why, as opposed to looking for a way to blame students for the issue. This is grounded in their extremely high degree of self-efficacy. Experts believe they make the difference in the classroom. This belief allows expert teachers to apply the why to students and to their own teaching.

Unlike the other teachers in the department, Mrs. Jones believes that when her students are struggling, she is responsible for working with them to figure out why they are struggling and then to develop and try solutions until they are successful. Mrs. Chin saw the process in action and believed it to be magic, yet it was the result of many hours of planning, processing evidence, and developing expertise.

THE EXPERT TEACHER THINKING PROCESS

Expert teachers' ability to apply the Expert Teacher Thinking Process to quickly analyze and solve issues is one of the reasons students grow exponentially in their classrooms. When the process occurs quickly in the classroom, it often appears to be magical to some and a lack of teaching to others. The lack of linearity in the process makes it messy and difficult to place into a neat step-by-step routine, which also makes teaching people to develop expertise a complex process of continual professional learning and engagement with peers.

When planning lessons, the expert considers the long-term expectations and then the short-term expectations. Experts design the lessons, student activities, and work produced to primarily elicit feedback. In the example, Mrs. Jones had students talk in pairs so she could hear them talking through the solving of the problem. Whereas Ms. Chin would have had students simply work the worksheet in silence. Mrs. Jones was seeking feedback to understand why the students were struggling, thus created the partner-talk activity in order to gather verbal evidence. Ms. Chin was using the worksheet for additional practice and assumed this would solve the issues.

Targeted Feedback is the type of feedback used to guide the learning toward short-term goals such as a specific skill attainment or mastery of unit goals. Targeted Feedback most closely resembles what effective teachers and leadership would consider feedback. Yet, once again, the expert uses Targeted Feedback for a much deeper level of introspection. For example, Mrs. Jones guided Ms. Chin through the examination of the exit tickets to find any lingering misconceptions or weak understandings that needed shoring up the following day. Mrs. Jones looked at each individual exit ticket, but she also examined the exit tickets as a whole to find overarching misconceptions or weak understandings. From this, she sought to understand why these elements were present, before developing the next solution. The expert teacher always reflects on the current evidence to understand why the issues exist.

Expert Vignette: Norming Solutions

In Mrs. Jones's class, the strategies she demonstrated to Mrs. Chin's students have long become norms her students use to work problems. A critical difference between experts and highly effective to effective teachers is their ability to allow students to move from concrete strategies to norming the strategy as part of their overall learning habits. While Mrs. Chin's students were using the concrete questions to analyze the problems, Mrs. Jones's students were able to mentally use the questions at an almost intuitive level through much practice. Once students can successfully use a strategy seamlessly, they do not need to work through the concrete elements simply for the sake of doing so. Experts recognize the purpose of strategies is to teach students to think and solve problems, not simple to do the strategy.

The students demonstrated weaknesses in their conceptual understanding of linear relationships. Mrs. Jones not only taught her students to understand the foundational principles of linear relationships but also slowly built their conceptual understanding through Persistence Feedback. Through a portion of her class she called Problem Solving Workshop, Mrs. Jones implemented *Persistence Feedback*. During the first six weeks, Mrs. Jones did not give any points for the answers. In fact, she blacked out the answers with a marker! She evaluated the students' processes and would give each student one thing to improve for the next week. After a few weeks, she had students giving each other Persistent Feedback by assessing the work of peers and suggesting one thing to improve for the next week. By the end of the first quarter, all of Mrs. Jones's students could analyze complex problems, solve them, and write effectively about their work. Mrs. Jones understood these were complicated tasks and growth toward mastery would take persistence and time. She focused her efforts on the long-range success.

The reason Mrs. Jones's students did not struggle with the linear function unit review like the other classes is that, at the beginning of the year, Mrs. Jones understood how the linear function unit fit into the overall expectations of the entire course. She wove together all of the feedback to move students from one understanding to the next so they could persist to the ultimate goal.

Persistent Feedback is the type of feedback used to meet long-term goals and has the overarching purpose of changing the mind-set of students about their abilities and skills. This type of feedback is slow and progressively builds one piece at a time. Students are engaged in the setting of goals and the reflection of their progress toward those goals. The expert uses Persistent Feedback to slowly move the student toward mastery of conceptual content understandings, as well as develop and refine lifelong learning skills. Persistent Feedback is based on the smaller day-to-day learning and the short-term goals but is always focused on the students' progress toward mastery of the Whole Student Understanding. Finally, Persistent Feedback builds in students what the experts in the study stated as the big idea they wanted students to master from their class: persistence.

NOTE OF CAUTION

Mastering expert teaching takes time and focused effort on the part of all the learners in the classroom. There is no script to follow. The skills, actions, and processes of expert can be observed. What is seldom considered is how and why these teachers process and think about the choices they make in the classrooms. This is the key to understanding expertise. This process is highly engaged and bound in multiple complexities. Unpacking these complexities is the purpose of the rest of this book.

POINTS TO PONDER

- Experts seek to deeply understand why issues are occurring before creating solutions.
- Experts constantly collect various types and levels of evidence to understand why issues occur in the classroom and how solutions are working.
- Experts partner with their students on solving issues.
- Experts are able to solve complex issues in the classroom due to their highly developed Expert Lens and their Whole Student Understanding.
- Experts consistently rely on feedback, Nimble, Targeted, and Persistent, to shape the teaching and learning process.

Chapter 6

Creating Conceptual Mastery

Amanda loves to plan travel excursions. Her family and friends often joke about her spreadsheets and laminated schedules they have endured on various travels. However, a journey is exactly what teaching is like for the expert teacher. The expert has a vision of a specific destination for the class and for each student. The destination is learners who can think conceptually about their content, leverage strong learning habits as needed, and apply powerful social-emotional attributes in a variety of situations.

The expert understands this journey is with the whole class but also knows the needs of each traveler along the way. This clear vision of the destination is forefront in every decision the teacher makes. The journey the teacher and students will take together is highly student-centered and focused on a destination of exponential growth for the students.

The success of the journey is dependent on the elaborate analysis process experts use to understand, chunk, and piece together a journey that leads each learner to a destination of success. This pre-journey element is critical and often overlooked, particularly as the profession moves more and more toward canned programs and curriculum. Expert understanding comes from the deep dive into the curriculum and standards experts do prior and during the year. This analysis and evaluation process is more than simply planning.

A critical note of caution before proceeding into the section: please do not read the word "planning" and attempt to create quick-fix schemes from this work. The following discussion must be read with the understanding that planning for expert teachers is a complex, elaborate process of analyzing, evaluating, and making connections for students. Expert teachers do not simply fill out quick lesson plan worksheets and proceed to class. Expert teachers spend arduous amounts of time processing and creating the classroom experiences for students.

FOCUS ON CONTENT MASTERY

Conceptual Mastery is a threefold process where the whole student develops toward mastery in content, learning habits, and socio-emotional attributes. Mastery of the content means the learner has the ability to leverage knowledge at will and apply a host of skills efficiently to execute any process as needed. The learner ultimately has the ability to make connections across the subject and across content to make high-level connections to create new ideas. This level of content mastery is sought more and more as the rigor of standards increase. However, if students are to think and work at this level, the teacher has to also be able to work and think beyond this level of content mastery.

First, experts understand the difference between processes, skills, and knowledge and how each build toward conceptual mastery. A *process* is the overarching application of a variety of knowledge and skills to complete complex tasks. Processes work together in allowing the learner to demonstrate conceptual mastery. *Skills* are the smaller actions or steps learner weave together to create the process. *Knowledge* includes the facts and information about a subject.

Experts understand the differences and break these down based on their analysis of the conceptual expectations. Experts begin their analysis of a curriculum by understanding not only what students have to know and be able to do but also the processes and the interconnected requirements of the process.

For example, at the end of a Language Arts course, students may be required to read three cold complex texts from different genres and answer a variety of questions at different levels about the texts. Then the students may be required to write an argumentative essay using evidence from the texts to support their reasoning. The expert teacher understands this is a multidimensional complex process requiring students to conceptually make connections to produce something new in their argument.

ELABORATE PLANNING TOWARD CONCEPTUAL MASTERY

The focus of the expert teacher's elaborate planning is to understand all of the whats, whys, and connections, before the expert makes decisions about how students will accomplish the expectations. Nonexperts plan what will happen each day and then how it will happen. Experts plan based on the needs of the whole student, both individual students and the collective whole. Their elaborate planning is the key to achieving success (see figure 6.1).

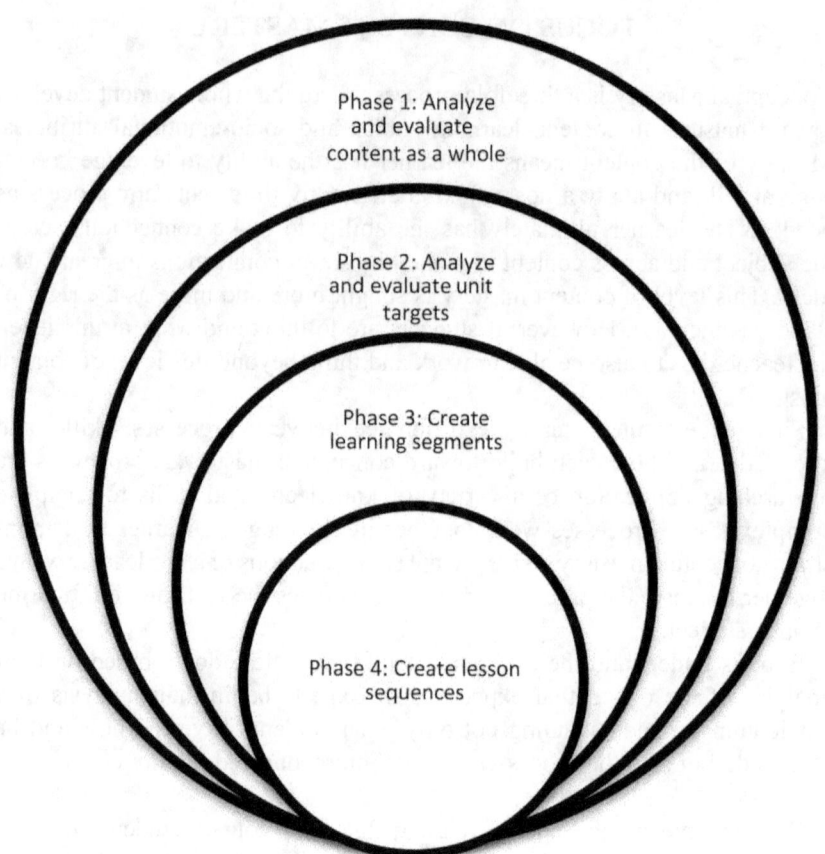

Figure 6.1 Elaborate Planning

PHASE 1: THE WHOLE

When planning toward Conceptual Mastery, the expert analyzes and evaluates the whole to conceptually understand what is required of students. This phase is a big-picture analysis and evaluation of the year as a whole. Expert teachers embrace standards as a roadmap for their journey. However, they do not embrace lock-step curriculum and the more increasingly prevalent scripted lessons, because experts understand each child is unique and each class is unique. Experts also know elaborate planning is key to their constant development of expertise.

The processing of the standards is what gives way to experts' deep representation of the content (Hattie 2003) and of students' needs. Experts do not work in a lock-step method in this journey but rather understand it so deeply that they can anticipate and adjust due to this deep understanding.

Expert teachers read the overarching standards as a whole and then read their curriculum from the end to the beginning several times looking for connections and cohesion. Experts ask themselves questions like:

- Why are these standards important?
- What are the overarching ideas?
- Why are these important to conceptual understanding?
- What do students need to know and be able to do to achieve content mastery? Why?

The analysis of the whole course is how the expert teacher is able to begin making connections, which will lead to the students being able to develop conceptual content mastery. Expert teachers connect new learning to prior learning; they preview the new learning and add narratives and anecdotes. They also introduce the content in small chunks in order to allow students to digest. These teachers are able to organize and teach the material in a way that students understand deeper meanings and make connections between content (Hattie 2010). The deep understanding within and across lessons is created by connecting information to big ideas (Good and Brophy 2008).

Experts also analyze the assessment expectations of students differently than nonexperts. Given the earlier example of the complex writing assignment, the expert analyzes the complexities of the conceptual expectation by actually working through a sample assessment. As the expert works through the assessment, the expert records all the elements required to successfully complete the task. See table 6.1 for a few example expert notes.

This ability to deeply understand the content, select the critical elements, and then weave together a year of learning to support the big picture ideas such as citizenship, lifelong learning, or effective communication was all exemplified in the interactions with the three observation subjects. Rather than teach simple skills or facts, experts focus on overall ideas students need to understand and create long-range plans for achieving the goals.

The long-range plan is based upon the overarching goals experts have about their course. For example, Abby, a middle school teacher, shared there were two ways to teach: *the easy way*, where a teacher gives students facts for the test on Friday, and the *hard way*, where the teacher maximizes students' learning.

The hard way is trying to get (skills/knowledge) hard wired into their heads. And getting them to use and read and stretch their minds and reading abilities and so all you need, as the teacher really, I believe in using lots of

Table 6.1 Expert's Notes

	Knowledge	Skills	Processes
Analyze text 1 (fiction)	Figurative language Background knowledge Plot Structure Vocabulary	Analysis of characters' actions/words Determine central theme Determine point of view	Inferencing Evaluation information from multiple sources Making connections between texts, to background knowledge, to inferences Organizing content to clearly convey understanding Writing for purpose with clear, individual voice
Analyze text 2 (information)	Fact versus opinion Relevant evidence Vocabulary	Determine central idea Make connections to analogies	
Analyze text 3 (poem)	Figurative language Inferencing Vocabulary	Determine central theme Analyze point of view	
Essay	Grammar Punctuation Writing styles Vocabulary	Create claims Create counterclaims Cite evidence Conclusions	

primary source documents. So we're not scared of (the curriculum), because we're already doing that; that's all we do. And by the end of the year they have read crazy stuff; actually it's from common . . . common . . . sense. (Abby, Middle School)

PHASE 2: UNIT ANALYSIS

Phase 2 of elaborate planning is understanding the mastery content targets expected at the end of each unit. Using their conceptual understanding of the whole, expert teachers reread each unit of the curriculum from the last unit through to the first unit. They analyze each unit to clarify the mastery targets, make connections between previous and future targets, and make connections to the overall Conceptual Mastery of each student.

From this analysis, the expert can move to Phase 3 (chapter 7) break units down into smaller chunks or learning segments that will eventually lead to the learning sequences of the day-to-day lessons. Experts know learning is a process, not a short set of simple targets to simply check off. They see the connections, both big and small. They also understand these targets vary in complexity and the time needed for development. For example, learning to analyze and find the central theme within a genre requires more than a short lesson.

When students are required to find the theme in different genres, the complexity increases. The expert uses students' previously mastered knowledge of theme to continually develop a conceptual understanding of theme as it applies to different genres. Eventually, students are able to make connections between any texts to universal themes.

Expert Vignette: Content in Connection to Conceptual Mastery

Amanda observed this lesson on a cold February morning as Fran's students gathered on the mat during the beginning of the lesson. Expert teachers are patient in the development of Conceptual Mastery. They possess deep knowledge of developmental stages and individual development, which is critical to their Whole Student Understanding. One example of Conceptual Mastery is the development of students' ability to gather, analyze, synthesize, and use knowledge and skills to create arguments. Fran, an expert first-grade teacher, demonstrated the development of conceptual mastery through the used daily writing activities to help her students move from being unable to write a sentence at the beginning of the year to writing multi-paragraph persuasive essays.

"Good morning! I am so excited to have you share your writing with each other today. I have asked two authors to share their work with us. Can someone please share with me what we will be listening for today as we hear these two essays?" said Fran.

"We want to hear strong persuasive language," said one student.

"We want to hear a claim with a purpose," said another student.

"We want to hear supporting details that connect to the purpose," said another student.

The students continued to review and Fran pulled up a list on the board to confirm what students were sharing.

"That is exactly what we are listening to hear," said Fran with a smile, as she invited the first author to sit in the author's chair and read her paper using a small microphone.

After the author finished reading, the other students turned to their peer partner and began to brainstorm what they heard in the papers that demonstrated excellence.

Fran said, "Now let's give one star and one wish."

One student said, "A star would be that the claim was very strong and I knew exactly what Annie's point was."

Fran wrote the point down by a star on the board, and then said, "Ok, can we now have one wish."

A student raised his hand and said, "Annie, you did a good job on your paper, but if you make your third point stronger, I think your paper would be better. You did not explain the third point like you did the other two."

The routine continued through another author sharing her work, and then the class made a list of things they could all use to improve their writing. Fran assigned a new prompt requiring the students to persuade a school committee which area was better for recess, the playground or the football field.

All twenty-seven students returned to their areas and opened their writing journals. They read their feedback, which had been given by either a peer or Fran. The students began their new work by reading their star and wish and making notes in their journals. Then they began working quietly and enthusiastically. A review of several journals revealed almost miraculous growth in writing over the year.

The first few pages of the journals were filled with misspelled, random works and pictures, whereas the current work was three- to five-paragraph persuasive essays with complex sentence structures. As they wrote, they shared their paragraphs with their peers for feedback and then rewrote as needed. This was done while Fran was working with a small group on a reading lesson. All students remained engaged and completed their writings. Fran later walked around and chatted with the students toward the end of the writings. She asked questions and noted elements in their work they may consider.

After class, Fran shared, "With our writing, I look at journals daily and I look at where they are and what do they need next to help them get better at their writing individually. I look in their writing journals to give those stars and wishes, which as you know, a teaching point and praise point basically individually in their writing conference. They start with what they did the day before; what they did today and what they need to get better for tomorrow.

As far as my class mini's lesson I kind of look at the overall. What does the class need as a whole? For example, yesterday they are able to show they know what an opinion is but they are having trouble writing and supporting, you know besides just giving me 'going to the park is fun.' (I want to know) why that is your opinion, so gives me some factual information."

Unpacking Conceptual Mastery

Fran's Stars and Wishes example defines the expert's ability to develop content mastery in students by focusing her Expert Lens on their writing development. The overarching goal in Fran's class is for students to be able to communicate, support, and share their ideas through various forms of communication with writing being one. The current unit focus was on persuasive writing and the day's lesson was focused on students being able to write and support clear opinions.

Fran's year-long understanding of where her students were headed was critical to the success of each day's lesson. Her Expert Lens is constantly focusing and refocusing on each student's progress toward mastery. However, she uses her pedagogical and interpersonal knowledge to constantly enhance the learning.

Pedagogically, Fran used the whole group discussion with the author's chair to refocus students on the important elements of persuasive writing as they reviewed through listening to peers what was important in their work. She also offered a very concise list of what their writing should include. Students self-reflected and used this list not only to refine their current work but also to build upon their conceptual understanding of how to communicate through effective writing. Fran purposefully developed students' learning habits in a systematic way that engaged both their peers (interpersonal skills development) and their intrapersonal skills of reflection and refinement.

The Stars and Wishes technique is primarily Target Feedback, but the peer-to-peer interactions in real time is an example of Nimble Feedback. Students receive daily evidence targeted on small elements of success and refinement. This pedagogical strategy is effective in not only building toward content mastery but also developing strong social-emotional attributes in the students. Effective teachers encourage students to reflect on their learning and to communicate where they are in the learning process (Marzano 2008). These reflective pieces, individual, peer to peer, and teacher to student, build toward larger goals.

Fran also used Nimble Feedback in the class discussion and as she later circulated throughout the classroom. Expert teachers allow students to have time to think through their new learning and make connections to prior learning through the multiple pathways (Marzano 2008). Each day students were offered one piece to celebrate and one small element to refine. The progress is slow but extremely purposeful and effective. This day-to-day interchange of Nimble and Target Feedback is what leads students to be persistent in their writing.

Another interesting element is how Fran engaged students in the entire feedback process to build their interpersonal relationship skills and strengthen the class culture. Students were highly engaged in listening to their peers read and thoughtful in their feedback. There was a sense that all were responsible for all. When working in pairs, the students were open in asking for help and in giving assistance. Despite Fran, often being on one side of the room with a small group, all students remained on task throughout the writing time.

Content-wise, the small daily doses of feedback helped students persist toward the overarching communication goals. Fran adjusted what she had planned for the day based on the discussions and work she had reviewed from the previous day's learning. Experts are more opportunistic and flexible in their teaching as they quickly use new information to bring new interpretations and representations of the problem to light (Hattie 2003; Shulman 1987).

This flexibility as opposed to the knowledge of possible scenarios makes the difference between experience and expert. Fran can then give the big picture Persistence Feedback on a unit writing piece and students are not overwhelmed, because the small elements have been refined along the way.

PERSISTENT FEEDBACK AND CONCEPTUAL MASTERY

The expert weaves into the course opportunities for Persistent Feedback as they move students toward conceptual mastery. Persistent Feedback is holistic, recursive, and gradual evidence focused on moving students toward conceptual mastery. Persistent feedback is evidence about the whole child's content understanding including knowledge, skills, processes, their use of appropriate strategies to learn, and their engagement in social-emotional attributes.

This holistic focus connects the expert's Whole Student Understanding with Conceptual Mastery to understand why misconceptions or issues may exist. For example, if a student is consistently struggling to make connections to math concepts while problem-solving, the expert holistically understands the student's math knowledge, their fluency and application of skills, and their ability to apply problem-solving processes.

Additionally, the expert will examine the strategies the student most likely chooses and how they engage with their peers during problem-solving discussions. Their inability to make connections between math concepts to solve complex problems is most likely a combination of content misconceptions and chosen strategies. The holistic nature of Persistent Feedback allows the expert and the student to examine all the elements and their interactions, before deciding possible solutions.

Persistent Feedback is also recursive in nature and continually builds toward the whole student toward Conceptual Mastery. For example, if a student is required to analyze various primary source documents to create their point of view for a debate, there are multiple skills and processes needed to be developed. The expert works with the student to continually refine each piece over and over through Targeted and Nimble evidence to build toward a strong debate. This view of the whole allows for the recursiveness to have purpose for both the teacher and the student.

Finally, Persistent Feedback is gradual and requires great patience. Fran did not look at her students' writing the first day and proclaim, "They should know how to do this already!" Instead, she assessed where they were and focused on where they needed to be in their abilities by the end of the year. She then chunked short-term goals and built-in day-to-day lessons, which moved the students incrementally toward conceptual content mastery.

OVERARCHING VISION

Expert teachers understand that deep, conceptual learning takes time and persistence. Expert teachers set high expectations and throughout the learning process remind students of the expectations, provide supportive feedback of students' progress toward the expectations, and guide students through constant adjustments without lowering expectations. Their ability to create and explain the deeper relationships of their subject to what is happening in the moment in the classroom is connected to their deep conceptual understanding of the ultimate goals.

Experts are able to detect, concentrate on, and give more instructionally significance feedback to students. They are able to make better predictions about possible misconceptions and create multiple pathways aligned to the needs of individual students to achieve success.

Hattie (2003, 6) states:

> I find it fascinating that experts take more time than experienced teachers to build these representations, have more understanding of the how and why of student success, are more able to reorganize their problem solving in light of ongoing classroom activities, can readily formulate a more extensive range of likely solutions, and are more able to check and test out their hypothesis or strategies.

As evidenced in Fran's classroom, the students of expert teachers are fully engaged in the consistent thoughtful discourse by sharing opinions and considering alternative solutions to various issues. Experts walk with their students through the learning process. They may lead when necessary but often are facilitating the learning along with the students. Sometimes the students may lead the facilitation, which strengthens their content knowledge, learning habits, and social-emotional attributes.

Note in Fran's classroom, students were able to not only write but also explain why things worked or did not work and then make suggestions for further development. This example is a perfect model of how Conceptual Mastery of the whole student develops. Fran's focus was on the positive development of the whole student: content mastery, learning habits, and social-emotional attributes.

Experts create student tasks, both formative and summative. They do so to provide deliberate practice focused on a clearly communicated criteria for success (Marzano 2008). However, experts are also developing learning habits and strengthen social-emotional attributes in students. Students are motivated to engage in deliberate practice and develop expertise because the purpose and the connections to the whole are consistently communicated.

Fran moved students incrementally by focusing everyone's vision on the overarching goal of conceptual mastery. Experts understand that students who achieve Conceptual Mastery are masters not only of content but also of learning habits and relationships.

NOTE OF CAUTION

Conceptual Mastery is the development of the whole student, which includes developing their learning habits and their social-emotional attributes, not simply mastery of the content. Because the expert deeply understands each student and their needs, the expert views the myopic-focus on single test scores to be limiting and defeating to students. The expert sees beyond single test scores to overarching goals for the student. This in part is what yields the exponential results in standardized scores; however, it is also what creates the disengagement and isolation of the expert during professional learning. The expert must discuss students holistically, not simply in terms of content mastery.

POINTS TO PONDER

- Experts process content over several iterations seeking to conceptually understand the content in order to make connections across the curriculum and across disciplines.
- Experts focus on making connections between content knowledge, learning habits, and social/emotional attributes as they analyze and process curriculum.
- Experts' elaborate planning process is recursive, purposeful, and reflective.

Chapter 7

Learning Segments

Experts are able to connect content to the larger contexts of thinking and learning. This is where their highly developed pedagogical knowledge is critical. Holistically, the expert understands how students learn and maximizes this knowledge in order to maximize achievement. Experts combine their pedagogical knowledge with the evidence they gather with the student to choose strategies to not only increase content mastery but also develop learning habits.

Learning is not simply memorizing facts and dates but rather making connections as we move from the concrete to the representational to the abstract levels of concepts. This process is not linear but rather recursive and requires multiple experiences in a variety of contexts and complexities. For example, a toddler is able to analyze what is placed on a plate and make a decision about whether to pick up the carrot or apple, but this ability does not demonstrate mastery of analysis and evaluation.

Rather, thinking must be modeled, scaffolded, and practiced throughout our lives as we become more and more purposeful and precise in our thinking. Experts know which strategies and tools each student needs in each type of context to manage the complexities. Experts understand thinking abstractly begins with concrete strategies. They are able to set the abstract concepts as the target and use the concrete to move students toward the target.

Experts use a variety of teaching models to engage students in thinking. The debate between such things as inquiry and direct instruction is not an issue in the expert's classroom. The expert uses all modes of instruction, not because of what is in vogue but because of what the experts understands about the development of Conceptual Mastery. The expert focuses on understanding why through the use of evidence and then chooses the how.

ELABORATE PLANNING TOWARD MASTERY

Expert teachers plan units beginning with the last unit through to the first unit. While units may be predetermined by state and local entities, the expert sees units as the encasement of the short-term chunks discovered when they were analyzing the why, what, and hows of conceptual mastery. In addition to strong content knowledge, expert teachers understand how students learn and how to teach students to become learners. Often teachers focus on the teaching of strategies rather than why a specific strategy should be used to teach thinking.

Pedagogical knowledge is often described as the quick-fix strategies teachers employ to help students quickly "master" a topic. Examples range from quick-fix writing strategies with short acronyms to finger-counting strategies for multiplication. While these strategies have purpose in the initial phases of learning, nonexpert teachers struggle to move students past these strategies to conceptual learning where students learn independently. However, the expert teacher's pedagogical knowledge is based not only on strategy but also on developing students' ability to think and learn independently, regardless of context. Experts develop students' learning habits through focusing on short-term chunks and targeting the evidence to meet the goals.

PHASE 3: THE UNIT TO LEARNING SEGMENTS

Experts plan the unit by focusing on short-term chunks designed to support the achievement of Conceptual Mastery. By planning the last unit first, then progressing backward until they reach the first unit, the experts create a cohesive yearlong plan with short-term checks and balances. They understand when a skill must be mastered and when a new skill should be introduced. They know what background knowledge is relevant and when new knowledge should be introduced. They understand what strategies may be needed to help students and how to know when to introduce them. They understand how each part fits into the whole, because they understand the whole student and Conceptual Mastery.

Unit planning occurs prior to the course being taught. Experts understand the overarching processes needed to achieve Conceptual Mastery and work to outline the critical learning segments on unit analysis from Phase 1 and Phase 2.

In Phase 3, expert teachers reread the individual units from the end to the beginning several times looking again for the connections between the units and for the cohesion to the Conceptual Mastery required of the whole year (see figure 7.1). As expert teachers design the unit, they keep the conceptual

Learning Segments

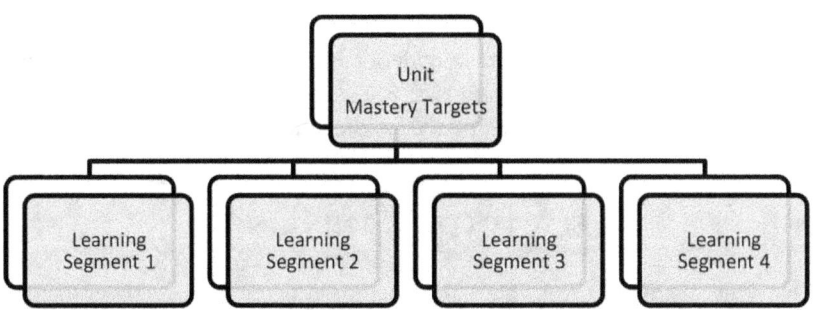

Figure 7.1 Phase 3: Planning

elements from Phase 1 and Phase 2 in mind as they analyze through specific questions and begin developing the smaller chunks they created.

Beginning with the last segment of the unit, the expert connects each learning segment to the mastery targets of the unit.

The expert is able to create these short-term segments of mastery due to their deep understanding of what is required for students to achieve Conceptual Mastery. The expert is then able to focus on short-term segments and design strings of learning experiences focused on the mastery of the short term. The segments are both whole units and smaller sub-elements. These include not only the short-term mastery of content but also the strengthening of learning habits as students apply various strategies to become independent thinkers and learners.

The expert begins the unit by explaining the short-term targets and showing students what mastery looks like for the unit. This concrete visual helps students understand the short-term targets and will be used throughout the unit as a guidepost to where students are in their progress toward the target. The expert can then work with the students to create goals and next steps as they progress toward the short-term mastery.

As previously stated, nonexperts plan the day-to-day activities of the class one day at a time with no focus on the whole. The expert plans for evidence of learning. When creating unit plans, the expert focuses on creating formative assessments with clear focus on the specific segments students need in order to reach mastery in their development toward Conceptual Mastery. These chunks are focused on content knowledge, skills, and processes, as well as on learning habits.

These assessments create opportunities for Target Feedback, which focuses on the broad elements needed to master the short-term targets through recursive engagement with students in a process of reflection and refinement. Experts do not simply pull an exit ticket or a quick quiz but rather create opportunities to gather evidence in partnership with students to understand where a student is in developing knowledge, skills, and processes, understand the why behind any misconceptions or issues the student is experiencing, and what strategies work most effectively for the student.

SCAFFOLDING THINKING

Whereas nonexperts focus solely on the daily objective, the experts focus on developing students who are independent learners and thinkers. This is done through teaching students to think using a scaffolding process. Experts are able to clearly model thinking processes for students within any given context. This ability to model thinking is the first step toward students growing metacognitively.

The expert then will use a variety of strategies to help students practice thinking in a scaffolded manner until they can process on their own. Experts facilitate students to make connections to their background knowledge as a foundation for learning new skills. They understand what each student knows and has mastered and uses this to build new understandings. The scaffolding is individual and focused (Good and Brophy 2008).

Expert Vignette: Scaffolding Learning Segments

> Fiona, a high school biology teacher, understands her historically low-performing students struggle due to a lack of background knowledge in science. A new conceptual curriculum has only highlighted their already-limited knowledge and skills. The short-term chunk requires students to read multiple texts and create an argumentative essay concerning environmental issues.

> I began planning units as a whole from the end of the unit backwards to understand the final expectations; keeping in mind the rigor of the curriculum along with the assessment requirements. However, the most important element in planning is where my students are in the progression of the learning. My kids have not had a consistent science teacher since the third grade. Now they are in ninth grade and the curriculum is tough. They are missing very basic vocabulary, both scientific and other, and their reading skills are significantly below average.

> In every lesson, I have to think about how I am going to bring the level of thinking required to understand the content, while I scaffold strategies so they feel safe to engage. Scaffolding the learning is critical, to meet the needs of a very diverse group of students. I have to think innovatively about how I structure not only lessons, but the units and the course as a whole. Everyone has a unique entry point, but all have to meet the same end goals.

In a recent lesson, students were required to read about current environmental legislation being debated at the national level and then formulate arguments for or against the legislation based on their knowledge of the interconnectivity of the various systems involved in climate science. Scaffolding the lessons over several days was critical to success.

Fiona continued:

I knew they had to engage with the text and I knew the complexity would scare them. So I chose the strategy, *I Notice and I Wonder* (Venables 2011), to help students consider what they already knew, brainstorm ideas, and explore solutions all within a comfortable, flexible and secure environment. Students worked in small groups initially with different pieces of text then shared out their notice and wonders with the class. This allowed me to model organizing the information.

Since there is no "wrong answer" students have a sense of empowerment because they can concretely see their thoughts are important and have a place in the greater discussion. Several students shared their notice and their wonders, in order to share, debate, and discuss their conclusions from the readings in a non-threatening manner. Additionally, the strategy allowed me to monitor and refocus their thinking as needed before moving to the next element.

Each group was required to find consensus about their view of the legislation. Fiona used a second strategy, *Placemat Consensus* (Bennett and Rolheiser 2001), which requires students to brainstorm, write their own statement, and come to a collective agreement as a group. This strategy allowed students the opportunity to accept, reject, or compromise on their initial understandings to ultimately reach a consensus.

She shared, "As students' conceptual understanding developed, their interpretation of the natural phenomena of climate change began to assimilate with the readings and data. They began to process and make connections as they exchanged their basic understandings of various isolated systems for a more developed conceptual mental model of the integration of systems."

Fiona continued:

I choose strategies that pushed students to evaluate and synthesize new content with their initial mental models of understanding. Such strategies are innovative because science in our district has primarily consisted of memorization of vocabulary and recall assessments. Students are not accustomed to reading complex texts, synthesizing those, and drawing their own conclusions with supporting evidence.

When I introduce such lessons, I have to find strategies to support not only the development of the science concepts, but also the development of metacognitive modeling and their thinking. *I Notice and I Wonder* is an example of letting students struggle through new content and make connections to emerging understanding. The strategy allows my more advanced students, who had met the target, to develop deeper conceptual knowledge through more rigorous texts and deeper wonders, while my other students build upon their limited knowledge through texts and Notices and Wonders.

> Fiona continued, "I believe solid strategies allow everyone in the class to have a voice, while holding each student accountable for engagement in the work. Each strategy requires students to apply their understanding from the leveled texts and engage in our discussions. I want them to learn to think and these strategies help them with a place to begin. By mid-term, we do not have to be as formal with our initial strategies as they simply begin all text by noticing and wondering."
>
> The last part of Fiona's discussion is key evidence of her expertise. Fiona recognized *I Notice and I Wonder* is a powerful strategy to teach students how to initially engage, connect, and think about the information found in text. However, the expert, in this case, Fiona, also recognizes the focus is not on the technical execution of *I Notice and I Wonder*, but rather on teaching students to intuitively notice and wonder about any text.
>
> In the beginning, students concretely write and share out their notices and wonders. In part, so Fiona could monitor their thinking and in part, so they can hear others' thinking. However, as the course progressed, noticing and wondering simply became a less-concrete part of the expectations for reading and thinking about what they read.
>
> Fiona shared that she slowly withdraws the concrete elements and helps student embed making connections to text into their learning habit toolkit. Fiona has a conceptual understanding of how independent thinkers and learners engage with new information. She used the strategies to concretely model this, but then moves her students to a more conceptual understanding.

Whereas the nonexpert will always require students to respond in rote manner using *I Notice and I Wonder*, the expert understands such a strategy is a concrete model of an abstract thinking process. Experts teach understanding learning strategies are really about teaching abstract thinking processes, not about memorizing a strategy, which is evidence of Fiona's expertise.

TEACHING REFLECTION

Learning habits depend on students being active participants in their learning continuum. In the nonexpert's classroom, there are smart students and there are the others. The smart students are the ones who know the material already and the others are the ones who do not. Statements like "They should know this already" are often heard from the nonexpert. This perception impacts students who often believe that the smart kids just know things as if by magic.

A nonexpert gives knowledge to students and then bases their scores on their retention of the knowledge. For example, a nonexpert will teach three-digit by three-digit multiplication on Monday, then assign practice worksheets each day of the week, and then give a test and record students' scores. The nonexpert may send home notes about working on multiplication, but little effort is made to engage the students in the misconceptions or issues in processing.

The student either can or cannot multiply. In English, the nonexpert will teach theme and assume that if students can define the term and find a general theme in one story, they have mastered the concept. There is a lack of understanding about how important reflection and refinement are to learning, which is a very recursive process.

Experts are highly reflective and flexible learners, who set short-term goals and concrete action steps to achieve these goals, because they understand the recursiveness of learning. Experts will spend large amounts of time gathering evidence through various forms of feedback to understand why students are struggling. The expert will include the students in the reflection process about their work.

From speed drills to self-reflection tools, the expert demonstrates how to reflect and understand why students are struggling, in order to help students, improve fluency and develop conceptual understanding of multiplication. Experts are transparent with students about where they are in the continuum and engage the students in developing a plan of action to grow toward mastery.

Expert Vignette: Growing toward Mastery

> Susan, an expert math teacher, sets a target for students to be able to multiply with fluency, multiply larger numbers with precision, and apply conceptual understanding of multiplication to complex problems. She also understands their conceptual understanding of multiplication is critical for their future success conceptually understanding algebraic concepts. Susan also knows learning habits, such as reflection and stamina, are critical to students persisting toward mastery.
>
> In the beginning of the multiplication and division unit, Susan and her students discussed their limited fluency of multiplication skills. Understanding that this small element would completely derail the students' ability to achieve the short-term unit target, the class discussed possible solutions. Susan believes when students set goals, monitor, and reflect on their progress, they will persist toward mastery. They create a system to address the fluency issue.
>
> My students take little multiplication speed drills every other day. It is funny to me how excited they get about these things. I hated them when I was a kid.

Anyway, what we do is the first drill of the year is the baseline. All you have to do is improve by one point the next time to get a point. So, if you have 10/70 and you make an 11/70 or a 15/70 you get an improvement point. That initially motivates them to try.

What really changes things is how I teach them to reflect on their drills and set a goal. For example, each student is required to look over their drills for the week and find what they are consistently missing. Let's say a student is missing questions with multiples of 7. We work together to make a plan and focus only on 7s. I usually ask the student to set a short-term goal like doubling the number of multiples of 7s questions they get right. Then we create an action plan . . . maybe the student will use flashcards to practice at home or they will work with a partner in class. I will also pull the student and we will do some hands-on work with multiples of 7. The next week, the student focuses on the problems with multiples of 7s. They meet their goal, which is so rewarding.

We set class targets for each month and then the ultimate target for the year. Students really want to see everyone reach the target. This works every time! They grow and they are amazed at how reflecting and focusing on one small element changes their knowledge. More importantly, they can use multiplication fluently in any situation from solving basic problems to more conceptual problems.

> The process of engaging students in analyzing and reflecting on their own work is a critical learning habit. Teaching them to set goals based on Target Feedback is critical. All too often students are simply given a grade without any sort of connection between the actions and the outcomes. Experts engage students in an active culture of being goal-setting, reflective learners.

An expert teacher's ability to be a reflective problem solver sets them apart from their peers (Hattie 2003). The expert teacher seeks further information with the student as a partner, whereas the nonexpert teacher focuses more on directly available data. Target Feedback focuses on collecting evidence about knowledge, skills, and processes that may prevent students from achieving the short-term targets. The expert is driven to solve problems with respect to individual students' performance in the class and collects individual evidence with precision, whereas the nonexpert teachers generally focus their decision on the entire class.

Expert Vignette (Continued)

> Susan also noted that the majority of her students struggled to understand what complex problems were asking the student to do. First, she had two students, who were not struggling, to work a few problems and think aloud as they processed the problems. Then, she asked several struggling

students to work through problems and think aloud as they processed the problem.

Afterward, Susan compared and contrasted the thinking of the two groups of students and realized the struggling students had a misconception concerning vocabulary that pointed toward multiplying. The next day she targeted vocabulary used in complex multiplication problems by grouping similar problems together during problem-solving workshop time, where students worked in small groups.

As students began to see patterns, they made connections and began increasing their understanding of how vocabulary cued them about what needed to be solved. Students worked through the model for several days with Susan engaging them in collecting evidence or Targeted Feedback about their successes.

When Susan recognized there was an issue with the majority of students understanding what the problem was asking them to do, she created a very precise method for collecting further evidence. She looked not only at the struggling students but also at the students who were successfully solving the problems. She was looking for why students were struggling as opposed to their wrong answers. Experts use Targeted Feedback to engage students in the process of learning as opposed to the results of a single answer.

Expert Vignette: Teaching Independence

Experts strongly believe in teaching students to think critically and independently. Experts do not teach what to think. Experts believe creating independent thinkers is the purpose in teaching students to process, analyze, and evaluate information. Experts believe teaching students to make connections and delve deeper is purposeful and creates Conceptual Mastery.

In Abby's middle school history class, the students read difficult historical primary sources, analyze, and connect the material to support their ideas. Abby is not looking for a simple answer on a multiple-choice exam but rather that students can read and think in a complex manner. She wants her students to be independent and to have confidence in their abilities.

Abby was introducing the ideas set forth in the Monroe Doctrine of nonintervention and non-colonization to her students. Knowing the Monroe Doctrine is a difficult text for seventh graders, she scaffolded the analysis of the document by building on students' knowledge of previously learned vocabulary and making connections to their understanding of prior events.

Abby began the discussion by sharing with students, "What are we going to do about that? John Adams put together a speech for Monroe that outlines what we're going to do. You have most of it in front of you. It's a little tough. You will help each other understand this. But to give you an overview, I want to show you the two main ideas of the Monroe Doctrine: (1) Non-intervention. (2) Non-colonization."

Abby then revealed two pictures, shown in figures 7.2 and 7.3.

Students then worked in pairs to analyze and draw conclusions about the pictures. After a short discussion, Abby facilitated students as they

Figure 7.2 Non-intervention *Source*: Mayeaux, Amanda. 2013. "Motivating Teachers towards Expertise Development: A Mixed-Methods Study of the Relationships between School Culture, Internal Factors, and State of Flow." Lafayette: University of Louisiana at Lafayette.

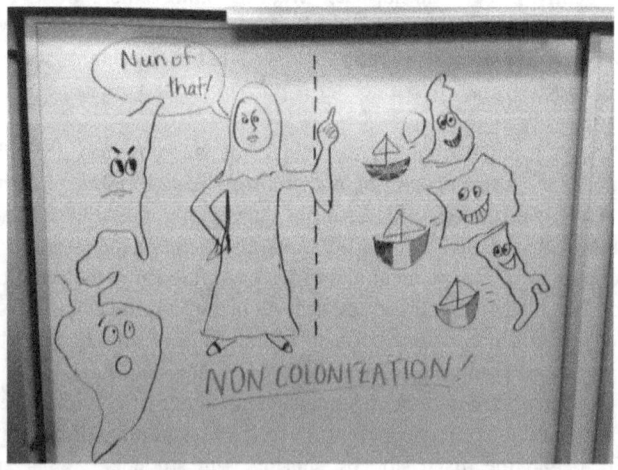

Figure 7.3 Non-colonization *Source*: Mayeaux, Amanda. 2013. "Motivating Teachers towards Expertise Development: A Mixed-Methods Study of the Relationships between School Culture, Internal Factors, and State of Flow." Lafayette: University of Louisiana at Lafayette.

deciphered the Monroe Doctrine. Abby moved from student to student using Nimble Feedback to guide the learning. Abby asked students to consider past and current events, which may connect to the Monroe Doctrine. She pushed students to connect with the historical texts, make connections, and then support their conclusions with evidence, and stand their ground for the discussion at the end of class, which lead to a lively discussion.

In the post-lesson interview, the discussion was an exciting part of Abby's reflection, "And so there's Demi, who has come to a conclusion based on evidence from the text that she thinks contradicts Quincy's and she's the only one back there. He's like, 'I don't agree!' And everybody else was like this and there's Demi . . . and she wasn't just like going along with the crowd." Abby shared that was the best moment, because Demi was thinking for herself and standing her ground.

Experts seek to create learners who are confident in their abilities to think and communicate their thinking. Experts focus on creating lessons where students must think deeply to understand the content, select the critical elements, and then weave together a year of learning to support the big picture ideas, such as being able to think critically and independently. Experts focus on overall learning habits and create situations where wins occur repeatedly in order to enforce these ideals.

Expert Vignette: Teaching Persistence

Amy, a middle school humanities teacher, said:

My students come to me not really enjoying reading. Before me they have been in many classes where someone read to them or they simply listened to books on tape. Teaching them to persist through a book is tough. I do all sorts of things to engage them. But ultimately, I teach them to set goals, create small action steps, and then read. We reflect and refine, until they are reading independently.

My favorite part of the year is when my most reluctant reader finishes the first book they have ever read independently . . . or when they finish their twenty-fifth book of the year. They are just in awe that they are readers. It is a wonderful feeling to know you helped them learn to push through and grow.

Persistence is always the ultimate learning habit for expert teachers. They use feedback to establish, monitor, and grow students to be resilient and persist. Experts understanding difficult tasks require stamina. Unlike nonexperts, who view feedback as a score or a grade, experts view grades as the very lowest form of feedback. A grade does not explain what is correct or incorrect. A grade does not explain what the student has mastered or misunderstood or why. Additionally, a grade given after the learning cycle has been completed is seldom effective in changing the learning. Grades are incomplete surface-level feedback and seldom yield any type of change in student learning or growth toward mastery.

The expert understands learning is about constant reflection and growth in order to persist toward mastery. In the expert's classroom, learning is fluid and ever-developing. Persistence is a multidimensional habit, which requires the learner to know where they are in the learning continuum, where they have to go, the steps to get there, and how to monitor progress along the way. The expert recognizes each student is at a specific place in the continuum of learning and partners with the student to push the learning forward to mastery. Teaching the student to persist toward mastery is one of the critical learning habits experts instill in their students.

Strengthening Learning

> *Stick-to-it-ness, you know, perseverance and in everything they do [you see] self-confidence. I want them you know [to learn] the lifelong skill of learning; perseverance, rigor is not a bad word; it means a little bit of discomfort but through that discomfort comes learning and then eventually comes confidence because you've proven it to yourself.* (Jan, middle school math)

The purpose of education is to create independent thinkers and learners, who have the skills and knowledge to maximize their potential, be active and independent citizens of society, and pursue their own happiness. Critical to these pursuits is the ability to think and to learn. Experts teach students how to think deeply and how to learn independently. Pedagogy is simply the methods teachers use to teach how to learn. The expert teacher believes the process of strengthening learning habits is a life endeavor. They also understand they are simply a piece of this process and seek to maximize the time they have with students to strengthen learning habits.

As expert teachers create and set high content expectations for their students, they also choose strategies to enhance their students' learning habits. In the expert's classroom, the Expert Lens is focused on thinking and learning rather than simply performing for a grade.

NOTE OF CAUTION

Experts' ability to chunk the curriculum and weave together the pieces into a cohesive whole is grounded in their elaborate planning process. This process is not a quick-fix, fill-in-the-lesson plan-worksheet type of planning. Experts spend hours upon hours processing and planning prior to students beginning classes. Experts reflect during lessons and after lessons on how to adjust and refine the planning.

Learning Segments

While experts will have the year planned out prior to the beginning of the classes, they are always examining how to improve learning for their students based upon their developing knowledge of the student. Because their understanding of the curriculum is so complex, they can focus on understanding the students. When teachers do not receive their curriculum in a timely manner, which is at least a few months prior to teaching the content, they are at a significant disadvantage. When states or districts choose curricula or when the school begins or creates the curricula one unit at a time, doling it out to teachers as they are teaching, the expert is frustrated and unsupportive. If systems desire to be expert systems, all pieces must be in place to support the experts and the development of expertise.

POINTS TO PONDER

- Experts segment units into logical chunks to develop Conceptual Mastery of each student.
- Experts use the segments to scaffold learning and thinking across the unit and the year as a whole.
- Experts build students' learning habits and social/emotional attributes in conjunction with their content development by focusing on reflective practices, independence, and persistence.

Chapter 8

The Day-to-Day

But I think to me the most important thing is that they know they are cared for and loved. They know that for forty-two minutes that day they're going to be in a room where someone loves them and cares for them and is worried about them and wants to see what's best for them. Most of the time, especially the message is just to learn, but if you know of the issues in their lives or whatever it is, they come first to me and you know I think that's . . . that's what motivates me, is them knowing that they are cared for and knowing that their needs are met. (Amy, seventh grade)

ENJOYABLE LEARNING

Expert teachers make learning enjoyable, which is very different from the fluffy fun observed in nonexpert classrooms. Expert teachers have a deep understanding of students' social-emotional needs and use this understanding to create enjoyable but rigorous lessons. Expert teachers use various techniques to engage students, which lead students to make connections, think deeply, and engage in the learning. Experts know three things about learning.

First, humans are curious creatures and we will seek learning when we are intrigued. When creating lessons, expert teachers consider ways to create curiosity in their students. For example, the expert may end the previous class with a question students are left to ponder. The expert may leave curious items on their desks and ask them to think about how these items may connect to the next lesson. The expert may read part of a chapter and then leave students hanging at a critical juncture in the story to entice them to read the rest independently. Experts are focused on what would intrigue students about a lesson.

Second, experts know learning is all about making connections to our background knowledge and experiences, between ideas, between content, and to our everyday lives. Experts create intrigue through connections. For example, for students to create a visual understanding of magnitude of number, they may work through a problem where they find the number of blades of grass on the football field. Throughout the year, students can connect to this image as they discuss tremendously large numbers such as the national debt in terms of numbers of football fields or the size of a single atom in relationship to multiple fields. An expert may begin a lesson about recycling by stacking bags of recycling materials collected from their home over the course of a week and ask students to estimate the length of all materials over the course of a year.

Finally, humans learn more when they enjoy the experience. Enjoyment is not fluffy fun and purposeless projects. Enjoyment is evidenced by students engaging and struggling with difficult concepts. What creates this enjoyment are the connections students make during the learning, the satisfied curiosity the learning brings, and the belief that the learning is progressing the student toward success. This constant building of social-emotional attributes, such as self-efficacy, bears tremendous enjoyment, even in difficult tasks.

For example, nonexperts will constantly share how students refuse to read or refuse to push through difficult problems. Conversely, experts share how they have never had a student not enjoy reading or how their students love challenging problems. The experts were not simply given all the best students; rather, they create lessons where students enjoy deep, rigorous learning experiences. These experiences are built upon the elaborate planning the expert uses to build the year and upon the constant reflection and refinement of the learning the expert uses as the year progresses.

PHASE 4: LESSON SEQUENCES

In 1982, Madeline Hunter developed a lesson plan model that would shift the view of what happened in the classroom for decades to come. Hunter's Seven Steps include: Objectives, Anticipatory Set, Teaching (Input, Modeling, and Check for Understanding), Guided Practice/Monitoring, Independent Practice, and Closure. The linear process was groundbreaking as Hunter introduced the concept that teaching and learning was a process of engagement between teacher and student, as opposed to the traditional structure where students simply worked quietly through a set of assigned material written on the board.

The issue is an example of what often happens in education; the model was consumed and misused as a quick-fix magic bullet solution to all that ails education. This basic model led to the creation of various lesson plan templates used across the nation. The foundation of Hunter's model is still seen throughout schools and preservice programs today. Yet the elements in the Hunter Model are some of the elements people use to learn. The difference is the elements are not strictly linear and, rather than a single input from the teacher and output from the students, true learning is a constant, recursive engagement of all learners.

Other theories of learning have held passing fancy over the decades from collaboration to Constructivism, but few have held as firm as the Hunter Model. First, Hunter Model works nicely in a linear lesson plan format. Second, the input-output element is appealing as it makes learning appear to be a simplistic exercise where an objective is shared, taught, and learned. Finally, the rote steps are easy to replicate, observe, and follow. If "teacher-proofing" every classroom is the goal, the Hunter Model is an excellent choice.

LEARNING AS A CONTINUUM

In the expert's classroom, learning is a recursive continuum that is built systematically and holistically. Expert teachers focus their Expert Lens on the content, the learning habits, and the social-emotional development of their students as they plan and as the lessons unfold. Their attention with the class is always focused on the students' needs, reactions, questions, comments, and interactions as they make adjustments throughout the lesson. The expert is able to flex and adjust due to their deep understanding of the learning continuum and the elaborate planning they have created. The continuum finally narrows down to the learning sequences, which are the short-day or multiple-day lessons that focus on the introduction, emergence, development, and refinement of new learning as shown in figure 8.1.

Experts know every classroom and every student are unique. Each requires a variety of experiences, structures, and strategies to successfully move students to achieve Conceptual Mastery. While the elements that Hunter defined certainly are part of the learning process, the process is not linear nor is it perfectly sequential. Learning is recursive and builds over time. Learning requires not only content focus but a focus on nurturing learning habits and social-emotional attributes. Learning that is emerging has different structural needs than learning that is being developed, refined, or reinforced.

This is where the experts are set apart. Their classes are designed for their specific students from their likes and dislikes to their strengths and weaknesses. The student is the nexus and everything is built around them. This hyper-focus on the students is one reason experts have such success with students, but it is also why they have a difficult time explaining their teaching.

The Day-to-Day 87

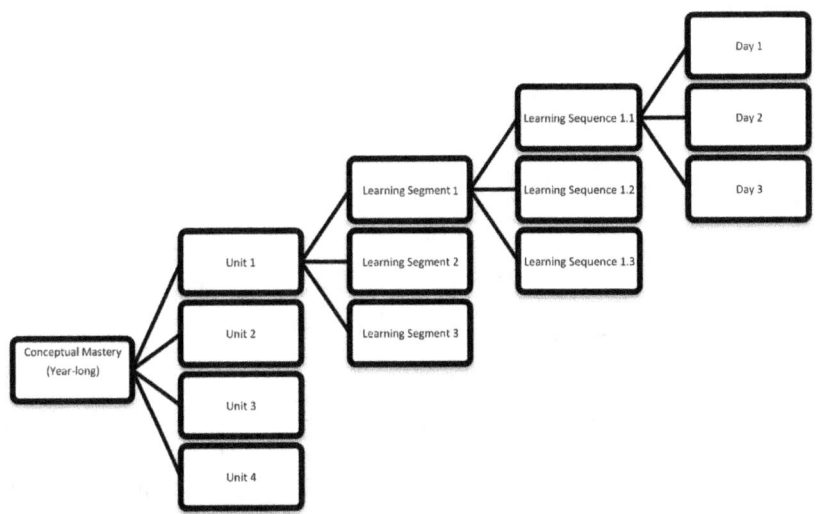

Figure 8.1   Expert Vision of Learning

Experts focus on the immediate context of their class. However, basic principles exist and can be used to further understand and replicate their thinking.

THE LEARNING SEQUENCE

In the beginning of planning the lesson sequences within chunks, the expert teachers develop a learning focus based on their Phases 1–3 processing. The learning focus is the combination of individual objectives students will develop over the course of the sequence to the point where the learning can move to a refinement stage within the next few sequences. A learning sequence may be a short as a single lesson or three to four days of lessons. The learning sequence supports the smaller chunks within each unit and is what experts use to create cohesion, as visualized in figure 8.2.

For example, in Language Arts, at the beginning of the class, students may engage in refining their work during writer's workshop where they work at their own pace on a long piece of writing as the teacher moves around meeting with students individually about their writing. Some students work on peer-editing with partners to discuss revisions and reinforce issues outlined in the feedback they have received. Then the students move to a whole group lesson where the teacher models an analysis structure for nonfiction text, before students work with partners to practice the analysis strategy using various levels of texts chosen specifically to meet their needs.

Figure 8.2 The Learning Sequence

Some students then apply the analysis strategy independently, while others work with the teacher to further develop the strategy. The teacher then wraps up this part of the lesson by allowing students to share their reflections of the effectiveness of the strategy in helping them understand the texts. At the end of the lesson, students engage in silent reading, while the teacher meets with students individually about their reading goals and efforts.

The learning sequence is centered on supporting students' progression of learning toward mastery of the objectives within the current lesson sequence, which then lead toward mastery of the chunk, then of the unit targets, and finally to Conceptual Mastery. Effective learning sequences require the expert to think systematically and holistically about what stage of the learning cycle students are in and what classroom structures best support students' development through this stage. Effective learning sequences also are designed to create multiple points of evidence for the expert and students to use to guide the development toward mastery.

Evidence

The expert begins with what evidence the students will produce for both the expert and students to analyze and use in their next step decisions during each stage of the sequence prior to actually creating the learning experiences. Experts spend a great deal of effort on creating ways for students to produce evidence of the progress toward mastery. Evidence may include not only written work but also all interactions from whole class to individual.

Experts create learning experience in the classroom in order for students to engage and produce evidence both collectively and individually. The purpose of evidence is to show where the student is in the process toward mastery. This evidence is used by the expert and by the students to make choices.

Evidence is not about grades but rather about reflection and growth. If the evidence is to be effective, whatever students are required to know and do must be distinctly aligned to the requirements of mastery.

Misalignment between mastery and evidence is often witnessed in nonexpert classrooms. The issue is threefold. First, nonexperts do not understand what mastery requires students to know and/or do. Second, nonexperts do not understand how individual learning objectives fit into mastery targets. Finally, nonexperts see student work as simple practice for a grade rather than evidence of progression toward mastery. For example, if the objective requires students to compare and contrast the point of view of two poems, the expert will build a lesson where students independently analyze two poems using previously learned strategies, focus the emerging learning on learning to compare and contrast the poems, and then have students write a summary supporting their conclusions with evidence from the poem using a previously learned writing strategy. The nonexpert will simply have the students complete a Venn diagram.

The expert teacher daily builds and reinforces the Teacher-Student Kinship not only to develop a deep understanding of the whole student but also to push the student toward Conceptual Mastery. This understanding is complex and individual based. The expert teacher is meticulous in the development of the relationship to not only understand the whole student but also have access to the evidence students will share in their discussions and work. The evidence informs the expert and the students about where their learning efforts need to focus next. What happens during the lesson to produce this evidence is dependent on the type of learning occurring and the needs of the students.

Ultimately, experts consider what students will be required to know and do independently to demonstrate mastery. Expert teachers provide multiple opportunities through various learning experiences for students to develop mastery. Experts also arrange learning experiences to create multiple, recursive opportunities to offer individual feedback, which Hattie (2003) suggests is the most important action a teacher offers in a classroom.

LEARNING SEQUENCES TO DAILY LESSONS

Each learning sequence is a puzzle-like combination of pieces that are connected to previous and future lessons. Experts consider where students are in the learning continuum for each standard and how these standards connect to the individual objectives within a learning focus. The basic elements of any daily lesson include introducing and/or developing of new learning, refining previously developed learning, and reinforcing foundational skills and processes. Each element requires students to produce evidence the expert uses along with the student to make next step decisions. Experts conceptually understand that these stages are not linear but recursive and build learning sequences to help students develop mastery (see figure 8.3).

New learning is often what teachers consider when planning the lesson. New learning is simplified to fit the Hunter Model style of teaching where teachers teach a single objective and students produce the single objective. Experts view the new learning differently. Experts consider all of the complexities of the new learning and how the new learning connects within the elements of the chunk and the unit as a whole.

During new learning, students need to engage without fear of failure or error. They need strong modeling of thinking and guidance in making connections. This is where new learning strategies can be introduced and/or previously learned strategies reinforced. In this phase, social-emotional attributes like self-efficacy begin to take root. Students need time to engage and wrestle with the new learning.

New learning is not introduced every single day and, when it is introduced, it is only a part of the learning. Experts design lesson sequences to purposefully allow students time to further develop the new learning to increase their understanding of mastery expectations and embed the learning more deeply.

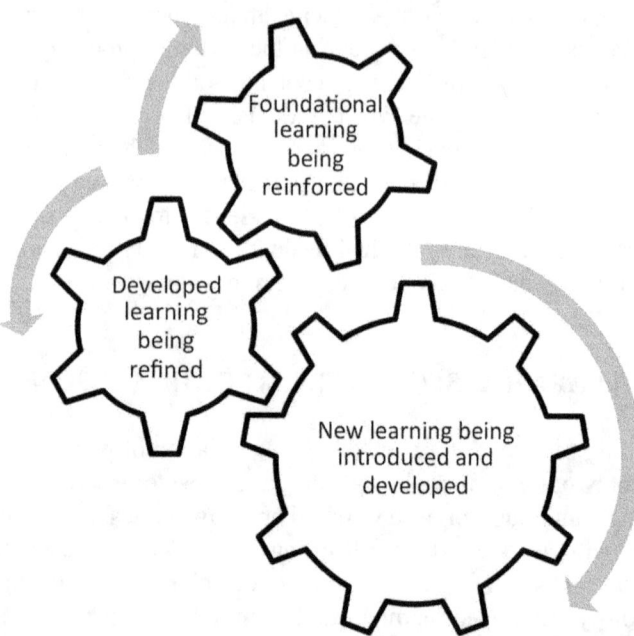

Figure 8.3 Lesson Elements

The development is where experts abandon the Hunter Model, because experts create lesson sequences where students develop the learning over the course of several days. Once students have a grasp of the new learning to the level of the learning focus, the learning can then become part of the ongoing refinement process.

Experts also create opportunities within the learning sequences for students to refine previously developed learning that has not yet reached the mastery level. Refining learning is particularly critical in pushing processes such as problem-solving or writing to the mastery level. Every day, students need time to refine learning from previous units and lessons and use their reflection skills to consider where they are in the progression toward mastery.

Reinforcement is the constant attendance to skills and processes critical to overall success. Reinforcement may be as simple as practicing foundation math skills to reinforcing reading fluency and comprehension through daily reading. Reinforcement is the daily calisthenics of the classroom.

When creating lesson sequences, expert teachers plan lesson sequences as a whole and arrange the elements in the most effective manner. Experts choose structures based on the learning focus, the needs of students, and their learning preferences. The structures are chosen to elicit evidence to help the expert and the students know where they are in the learning continuum. The structures are also chosen based on the particular characteristics and needs of the students as a whole class and as individuals.

Classroom structures break down into three specific categories: individual structures, group structures, and teacher actions. The structures are chosen and are not based on where they should fall in a linear lesson plan, but where they most appropriately fit to support students' progression toward mastery.

Classroom Structures

Experts use individual structures, group structures, and teacher actions to create lesson sequences to develop the learning. The structures within the learning experiences are designed to engage the expert and the students in the learning experience and to elicit opportunities for evidence to be produced. The expert is responsible for the overall facilitation of the experience and for specific teacher actions ranging from modeling to questioning. Students are responsible for fully engaging in the experience through the prescribed or chosen actions.

Independent Structures

While this element traditionally occurs at the end of most lessons, the expert may have students work independently in short time frames throughout the lesson. The expert places this element when and where it is appropriate for students. Independent work may be as simple as an exit ticket or as complex as a writing piece students complete over the course of several days. The critical point is that students are able to demonstrate mastery of the objective(s) and all the supporting pieces independently.

In nonexpert classrooms, the independent practice often does not meet the level of rigor required of the student by the standards. The work is simplified with little connections between previous and future learning. Ineffective independent practice is often considered "busy-work" and remains in a basket on the teacher's desk day in and day out. When independent practice is done with little to no feedback from the teacher, students practice skills and processes incorrectly, which further cements misconceptions.

Another issue is when the only time a student demonstrates independence is on the unit assessment and sometimes not even then. For example, a class of third graders is required to read two cold passages and find the connections between the themes of both pieces. In class, students are never required to read independently, as every story is read aloud by the students or read aloud via a recording of the story. For the test, the teacher has students answer questions about previously read stories.

In the expert teacher's classroom, students are independently reading cold passages on a regular basis. In previous lessons, the students learned a theme-analysis strategy and then applied it to analyze the two new stories introduced that day. After the teacher modeled, making connections about theme using previously read stories, students worked collaborative to make connections about previously read stories.

However, during their independent practice time, students read and analyzed two new stories. The teacher chose different stories at different levels for her students based on their need. Her focus was on students making connections between themes of two stories. Then students wrote a short paragraph explaining the connections between the themes of the story. The expert teacher used this evidence to decide if the smaller skills need refining.

Independent processing time allows the expert to engage in observing and working with individual students as needed. Independent processing is the time in the lesson when Nimble Feedback is critical to redirecting any previously missed misconceptions before these take hold and become a barrier in the student's progress toward mastery.

Group Structures

No part of the lesson is expertise more prevalent than in how experts effectively use group structures in their classrooms. Experts know learning is a social process, as well as an independent one. Experts leverage collaboration and interdependence to provide students with opportunities to develop and refine their social-emotional attributes, to build a strong classroom culture, and to support progress to mastery. Experts use a variety of collaborative structures to maximize learning in their classrooms. Experts choose collaborative structures based on the needs of students and on the match between the structure and learning focus. Group structures can be used during all stages of the learning continuum.

Group structures may be used to help students brainstorm new ideas or make connections to background knowledge. For example, at the beginning of a unit on the Renaissance, the teacher has students write down issues the Middle Ages posed for people. In small groups, the students decide the three main issues and make predictions about what will happen during the Renaissance to overcome the issues.

Group structures are effective when students are developing their learning. For example, an expert may use a partner talk structure to help students practice the step-by-step process of solving linear equations. The partner talk allows students to hear the steps from the partner and also direct the steps for their partner. During the practice, the teacher can walk around and listen as students walk through the steps, while using Nimble Feedback to correct missteps or misconceptions.

Group structures may be used to refine and to reinforce the work of students. Before turning in the first draft of a report, pairs of students are assigned an element to assess. Each pair reads rough drafts for their element and gives feedback to peers. As each report moves around the room, all required elements are assessed. After the feedback is completed, each pair makes a chart about the most noticed misconceptions and mistakes pertaining to their element. Not only are students more aware of the various elements, the teacher is also.

Group structures create opportunities for the teacher to really listen to students' discussions and processing. In nonexperts' classroom, student talk is seen as a negative without purpose. The expert uses group structures to efficiently and effectively understand where each student is and then applies Nimble Feedback to redirect as needed before the students move toward independent work.

Teacher Actions

The actions of the expert teacher in the classroom are purposeful and focused. Experts are highly engaged in every minute of the lesson, constantly scanning the whole class for evidence of learning, while also being able to monitor individual students. Teachers' awareness of the classroom has often been described as "with-it-ness" and seen through their proximity to students. However, at the expert level, the constant, agile engagement between teacher and students creates a focused awareness of where each student is in the learning process, thus providing Nimble Feedback between all.

Experts use a variety of teacher actions to maximize learning. In any given class, the expert exhibits a wide range of actions from modeling thinking to facilitating discussions to simply observing students as they work. Each action has purpose and is tied to the daily objective(s) and to the larger goals. The overt expert teacher actions that occur during classroom instruction may include direct instruction, modeling thinking and processes, facilitating the development of the emerging learning through group and individual activities, observing and collecting evidence about student learning, redirecting learning, and engaging students in reflection about their learning.

These actions occur both individually and simultaneously as needed. For example, an expert may be in the midst of modeling a strategy but is also scanning the room to observe students for their reception of the model. The expert is watching facial expressions, body language, and other signs of processing.

Observing expert teachers work is to see artistry in motion. In their mind is a basic visualization of how the lesson will progress, but there are also multiple contingencies they are prepared to manage based on the Nimble Feedback they receive from the students. This agility to quickly analyze evidence of learning from the student and make adjustments through redirection, questioning, facilitation, and observation is difficult to break down, because there are no set steps.

The expert is constantly aware and responding to the needs of the students. They are constantly collecting evidence to use in their reflection of the lesson and student learning. Experts will record these observations using various anecdotal note strategies, collect student work samples, and even record students discussing the learning. They are able to respond effectively and efficiently, because they have purposefully developed strong Teacher-Student Kinship and have a powerful Expert Lens.

They model these characteristics as they reflect and modify in their classroom. The expert's high level of flexibility is the key to the expert's ability to solve problems instantly in the classroom (Costa and Garmston 1998; Mayeaux 2013). Hattie (2003) supports the idea by explaining that experts are more opportunistic and flexible in their teaching as they take advantage of new information, quickly bringing new interpretations and representations of the problem to light. This flexibility through reflection is modeled and transferred to students in their classroom.

THE LEARNING SEQUENCE DEVELOPMENT

The development and implementation of the learning sequences is complex. Each piece of the learning sequence weaves together to connect to the chunk and to the unit as a whole. The rest of the chapter offers examples in how the expert teacher creates learning experiences that lead students ultimately to Conceptual Mastery.

Developing learning sequences is more complex than simply planning day-to-day lessons. The focus of how the sequence rests within the chunk and the mastery of the unit as a whole is critical. Experts also understand mastering knowledge such as types of poetry occur faster than mastering a process such as analyzing poetry. Experts also think through the pieces of a learning sequence by focusing on what emerging learning must be introduced, developed, and refined, while also refining and reinforcing previously mastered learning.

NEW LEARNING

Emerging learning is what most considers the heart of the lesson. For non-experts, these lessons are about new learning. Basically, the cycle happens with little connection to other lessons. Teachers teach. Students practice independently. Learning may or may happen. Students move to the next lesson. Teachers proclaim, "I taught it!"

Experts view new learning simply as learning that is new and emerging in connection to previous learning. Experts understand how prior knowledge, skills, and processes interconnect. They also understand how their students learn and seek to develop each piece of the lesson to maximize learning. Emerging learning is taught in such a way as to deepen the interconnectedness between the previous lessons and the future lessons.

When presenting new learning, experts focus first on guiding students to make connections to previously developed learning and then use appropriate strategies and structures to introduce the new learning to students. During both parts, experts elicit evidence to guide the learning.

The complexity of the new learning is also considered. New knowledge is often introduced to students through reading or viewing or may be conveyed through a lecture with students taking notes. Knowledge has a place in the learning.

However, the more complex learning of new skills or new processes require more planning and engagement. The expert must be able to clearly define expectations and deconstruct of the thinking for students to follow.

Expert Vignette: New Learning

Throughout the year James's students had analyzed various pieces of text; however, the new unit required them to analyze poetry. James suspected his students would struggle with this new process. Understanding that poetry analysis is complex, James evaluated what was required to reach the target and how to best scaffold students thinking toward the target. He then chose a strategy he felt would best support his students and designed a learning sequence to introduce the emerging learning.

At the beginning of the lesson, James had students work in partners to brainstorm all the clues they used to analyze other pieces of text in previous lessons, including elements such as figurative language, symbolism, and imagery. James wrote those elements on the board and had students share examples to help them make the connections. James then began to model his thinking about the poem and the analysis strategy using very clear and precise steps. First, he read the poem all the way through. Then he read it a second time, making connections and describing what he visualized in his mind.

"The darkest night, I walked alone along a winter's road," he read, "In my brain I see myself walking down a dirt road from my childhood on winter's night. The woods were so dark and I could see the eyes of animals looking at me. I can still feel the chill of the cold wind on my back."

James continued through the poem. Then he said:

> Now I am going to read back through the poem for third time and look for three elements: symbolism, imagery, and figurative language. As I find these, I am going to write them in this graphic organizer and note the connections I can make. When I reread the first line, I see the darkest night as maybe as a symbol for something. I was very afraid that night, so maybe the darkness with all of its unknown symbolizes fear. I am not sure, but this is what I first think about when I read it. The poet also uses the idea of winter and cold to highlight the desperation of the situation, so I write down fear as a possible idea connected to the symbols of night, darkness, winter, and cold.

James continued through the poem, noting when he found the three elements and the supporting evidence. When he finished, he gave students another poem and walked them step by step through the strategy.

As new learning emerges, making connections to previous learning and initiating the construction of new learning are key to students building a foundation toward mastery. Making connections to the previous learning helps students recognize where the emerging learning fits within the continuum. Making connections can be done in various ways. James used a group structure to have students brainstorm and make connections to previous learning. Engaging students in making the connections is more effective than simply telling them what the connections are.

Initiating the construction of the new learning may occur through various strategies and structures such as experiments or simulations. In this case, James chose to use modeling, which is a key expert teacher action during emerging learning. The modeling of thinking and of processes is critical to students being able to develop and refine the learning as they move from concrete understanding to abstract conceptual understanding. James did not tell students to write down a symbol, but rather modeled the connections he made in his mind to find possibilities for what the darkest night may represent. James's modeling of process over finding a correct answer demonstrates his expertise. He realized analyzing poetry is an individual process with various answers depending on the connections the reader makes.

Modeling is commonly called a think-aloud, because experts clearly model their thinking by sharing what is happening in their minds as they think through the process in focus. Whereas a nonexpert will simply state, "First read the poem, then find some words that are used a symbol. Write those words in the chart." James's model was completely different and focused on his thinking and how he processed and made connections. After reading the poem through and then again as he thought through the lines, he began to make connections for the students.

While modeling looks differently in various contents and at various levels, the focus is to clearly model thinking and processes so students can concretely see how abstract thinking works. Modeling is often misconstrued as lecturing. While lecturing has a small place in classrooms, modeling is a completely different teacher action.

Nonexperts will simply tell students what to do. For example, a nonexpert may or may not use a specific analysis strategy. If then they do their introduction and "teaching" of the strategy will be "Ok, read the poem three times. Then find the symbols, imagery, and any figurative language. Write down your examples and what you think it means. I am picking this worksheet up for a grade." Technically, the students are doing the same actions, but the focus is not on the thinking process.

Developing New Learning

Developing learning encompasses a larger chunk of the expert teacher's lesson sequence than the nonexpert teacher's lesson. Experts understand if learning is initially well developed, refining and reinforcing can focus on pushing students to more complex levels. Developing learning may be as simple as helping students remember needed knowledge to a student developing the skill of adding fractions to the complex process of writing to persuade.

Whereas nonexperts focus on rote memorization of knowledge, experts focus on developing students' skills and processes. This section focuses on both pieces separately to create a clearer understanding of how development of both works within a learning sequence. Skill development usually begins with a model and then students use the model to practice the skill such as analyzing a poem in James's class.

Expert Teacher Vignette: Developing Skills

After the model and group practice, James paired students to practice each step of the analysis strategy. James had chosen poems based on complexity to match students' reading levels. Each pair had a chart with the steps clearly outlined and space for them to record their thinking. As James saw evidence suggesting students were struggling, he used Nimble Feedback to redirect them and encourage them.

"Sam, are you struggling understanding this line?" James asked.

"Yes, I hate poetry, because I don't get it," said Sam.

"I will read the line to you and I want you to close your eyes and just listen," said James, "The long lonesome sound of the nightingale echoed across the field. . . ."

Sam said, "I don't know what a nightingale sounds like."

James asked, "When do you most often hear birds?"

Sam said, "Well, in the morning there is the really loud bird in a tree by my room. It's the only time I hear it."

"So, I want you to think about that and make a connection between why you only hear this bird early in the morning and how that may connect to quietness, echoes, and loneliness."

The expert understands students make different connections, because they have different experiences. Sam was struggling with analyzing poetry, because he had difficulty making connections to his own life. Despite the concrete strategy, James had to support a smaller piece of the lesson for Sam.

James's small refinement of Sam's thinking will help move him toward mastering the short-term chunk of analyzing poetry with a concrete strategy, then onto analyzing poetry in a more conceptual manner. Again, the understanding that the ability to analyze and abstractly understand poetry is the target, rather than simply learning a concrete poetry analysis strategy, allowed James to focus on small pieces of the thinking. This is evidence of expertise.

James's students will use the strategy over the course of several days to analyze more complex poems and begin moving toward being able to make connections between all types of texts to further develop their thinking processes.

Whereas skills may be introduced and developed over a few days, the development of processes takes long periods of time. Processes include such things as learning to write effectively for different purposes, reading and deeply comprehending various types of texts, reading for pleasure, solving complex problems, communicating thinking in multiple ways, and various thinking processes such as analysis, evaluation, and synthesis.

When creating time for the development of a process during a learning sequence, the expert considers where and when students are mastering the process, what they need to move progress, and how these needs fit within the context of the sequence. Sometimes the skills being taught apply specifically to an ongoing process such as James's focus on teaching students to analyze complex text.

However, sometimes the processes only somewhat relate to the specific focus of the sequences such as developing reading stamina. In the development of such processes, expert teachers often organized this part of the learning sequence using a workshop-style design. This design not only allows students to have time to work independently or with a peer as needed but also allows time for the teacher to work with students individually or in small groups. The style also maximizes the teacher's ability to support the individual student's needs. The workshop style of instruction is not a perfect fit for all types of instruction, but it works wonderfully in the development of complex processes. Additionally, it is one more tool the expert has cultivated and can use effectively in supporting students.

The nonexpert will simply have students continue to fill out the worksheet and then give students a test where they fill out another worksheet. The focus is on the rote filling of the worksheet rather than the thinking. The students never move toward the strategy becoming a process that is normed into their learning habits.

In the expert's classroom, once the new learning is developed to the level where students can use it to move to the next learning sequence, the new learning become the focus of refinement.

REFINING LEARNING

Refining learning is an ongoing process and different from development in that students have developed the learning toward mastery enough so they can use the skills and processes independently. However, their use of the skills and processes has not fully reached mastery level. Experts help students make connections across the year by constantly refocusing them toward mastery and refining their learning. For the expert, the learning is never done and can always be refined. Experts also understand that refinement may need to occur due to various things such as an increase in complexity of text or a newly developed strategy. Learning is recursive, which is most evident in the refinement elements of a learning sequence (see Appendix).

Refining learning allows students to experience that mastery of any learning is a process that requires engagement, reflection, and focused practice. Through the refinement elements of learning sequences, learners build stamina, make connections, and learn to reflect and focus on more than the right answer. They also begin the process of norming the strategies they have used to develop the learning.

Expert Vignette: Refining Learning

After the learning sequence where students used the poetry analysis strategy, James then modeled evaluation of their analysis to help them find themes. These two pieces were developed over the course of three days. Then refining the strategy into an intuitive process began. After a few days, James removed the worksheet with the chart of the analysis structure on it where students had written their evidence for each step of the strategy. Instead, James had students color-code each piece of evidence and then draw their own graphic to make the connections.

The students underlined examples of figurative language in red and circled symbolism examples in green. Once they could successfully analyze poems at various complexity levels using the strategy more fluidly, James allowed them to only annotate what they felt they needed to mark. Step by step, over the course of the unit, he removed the concrete pieces of the strategy to move them to intuitively analyze poetry as a cognitive process.

During the next unit, James was pleased to see how students used pieces of the poetry strategy to analyze some short stories and they began to make connections; thus, the strategy had become internalized and the process became normed. This focus on refinement from the concrete to the abstract is a model of expertise. Nonexperts do not make the connections between strategies and processes nor do their students.

REINFORCING LEARNING

Bell ringers, warm-ups, speed drills, journal writing, homework, and test-prep practice are all the hows of reinforcing and refining foundational skills. When nonexperts plan these, they look for a workbook with a daily set of quick work students can do while the teacher takes roll and gets set-up for learning or they assign mundane homework in a blanket manner to every student, regardless of need. This type of work is often referred to as "busy work" and yields little in the move toward mastery.

Experts view reinforcing learning quite differently. Experts believe that this part of the lesson is an opportunity to engage students in mastering basic knowledge and skills, to increase their ability to diagnose and solve their own learning needs, and to increase their self-efficacy.

Expert Vignette: Reinforcing Skills

Shannon recognized her science students were struggling to analyze various visuals on the ACT (American College Testing) the given time frame of five minutes. While she had created and taught them an analysis strategy for analyzing visuals, they were slow. To overcome this barrier, she created daily warm-ups focusing on this small element of the ACT. Initially, Shannon gave students four minutes to analyze the stimulus and then four minutes to answer the questions. Each week she shortened the time period until students could complete an entire passage in five minutes.

Shannon also engaged students in the analysis of the passages each day using Nimble Feedback. As students worked, she moved around the room and recorded what they were doing and how they were processing the information. After the time was up, students shared their answers, discussed their thinking behind their analysis, and focused on patterns they found in their errors.

Shannon did not review or assess the passages for a grade, but rather had students set a goal for a post-test at the end of a three-week cycle. If they achieved their goal, they earned twenty points. All students achieved their goal as the progress was individual and gradual. Shannon was also excited to learn several students began doing practices independently at home.

The process was applied to all areas of the ACT with great success in various classes. The use of Nimble Feedback was critical to students engaging in the process. By having students analyze the small chunks of work each day to find patterns in their errors, Shannon was able to help them focus on overcoming one error at a time. The high engagement in critical analysis of individual work builds a culture where error is embraced and used to learn. Additionally, as the students improved, their belief in their ability to learn and improve increased, thus increasing their self-efficacy toward ACT and also learning.

Expert Vignette: Reinforcing Foundational Skills

Amanda built a refinement process to help her students refine their computational skills with whole number, decimal, fraction operations to mastery-level fluency and skill. After noticing that number relations was an area of significant weakness for the majority of students, Amanda devised a pretest where students were required to add, subtract, multiply, and divide whole numbers, decimals, and fractions. Mastery was considered 80 percent in each subarea.

If a student did not meet mastery, the student then set goals and contracted to improve one area. For example, Ann only mastered adding and subtracting whole numbers and decimals during the pretest. She set a goal of mastering multiplying decimals. In her contract, she agreed to complete three nights of homework practice on the skills, participate in a peer-led small group lesson, and focus during daily warm-ups on this skill.

Each day, the students were given focused practice problems and worked with a peer partner to analyze their work for errors with a focus on their chosen skill. Students were very engaged and began to see results within the first round. Despite grades not being given, everyone engaged in refining their learning. Students also completed the homework as it had purpose and they had choice concerning when it should be done.

Throughout the year, the cycle was used to grow students' foundational skills through the daily practice and individualized homework. Because the students had choice about their focus, they were more engaged and felt in control of their learning. Additionally, students also embraced responsibility for their peer's mastery of the content. As more and more students reached mastery of all skills, they would reach out to those struggling to offer support.

Reinforcing skills in a purposeful manner engages students and builds their self-efficacy as they learn to analyze their mistakes and practice with purpose. Overcoming small foundational skills such as multiplication or spelling or vocabulary has to be done in a purposeful, short burst of practice method each day. When students see purpose and experience growth, this part of the lesson is no longer mundane or purposeless. The process also becomes foundational in teaching students to reflect and grow as learners. Finally, the process builds classroom culture where errors are welcome, but used to understand next steps, and where everyone supports everyone's journey to mastery.

THE LEARNING SEQUENCE IN ACTION

As the days unfold one after another, the elaborate planning process the expert used to design the year, then the units, then the smaller chunks, then the learning sequences, begins to breathe.

In a three-day learning sequence with a learning focus on adding fractions, students experienced a variety of structures and produced multiple points of evidence of their learning. On the first day, the class began with students working individually, then in partners to reinforce skills from a previous lesson that connected to the emerging learning to be introduced. The students gave feedback to each other and focused their discussions on what their peers did well and what they still needed to refine.

Then the teacher introduced the new skills through a whole class discussion where the students participated in a short brainstorming activity where they made connections to previous skills. The teacher then modeled the skill using specific thinking questions applied to examples. The students then worked as a whole group to practice the model before moving into a partner structure to further develop their learning. After a few minutes, students worked independently to complete an exit ticket to show their individual progress.

Finally, students moved into a problem-solving workshop structure where they refined their problem-solving skills by working on complex problems of their choice. While most of the students were in problem-solving workshop, the teacher worked with small groups on a mini-lesson reinforcing the previous week's lesson and discussing common misconceptions found on the assessment of the last chunk.

On the second day of the sequence, the students worked in partner groups moving through various stations designed to further develop and refine their mastery of adding fractions. The stations were set up to be fun and engage students in solving real-world problems, given various scenarios. The stations connected to an overarching mystery problem students were trying to solve. During problem-solving workshop that day, the teacher pulled a different small group to refine their problem-solving skills as she realized they were ready to be challenged.

On the final day of the sequence, the students engaged in a whole group game simulation, which required them to apply their mastery of adding fractions, plus other skills to solve complex problems to defeat the villain in the game. Problem-solving workshop was not held that day due to the game requiring a great amount of time. At the end of class, the students completed a short independent quiz that included multiple levels of problems that met the learning focus of the sequence, as well as some reflection questions about their experience. The students also submitted their work from problem-solving workshop for feedback from the teacher.

As the relationships grow with and between all the learners in the classroom, a powerful classroom culture, conducive to risk-taking and exponential learning, is created. Learning is always in focus as the teacher leads students toward Conceptual Mastery of their content, learning habits, and social-emotional attributes. The expert strategically builds and reinforces each piece, so the knowledge, skills, processes, and habits are deeply embedded into the learner. The expert understands, once these elements are deeply rooted, the learner will continue to use them to grow and develop well beyond their time with the expert (see figure 8.4).

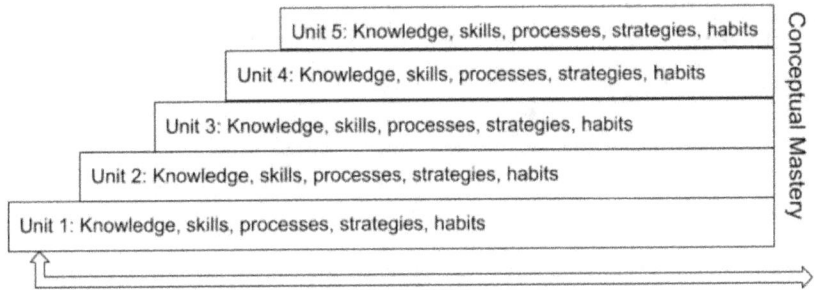

Figure 8.4   Expert Vision of Learning

This brings to full circle all of the actions, choices, and work of the expert back to Teacher-Student Kinship. The expert is deeply motivated to have a lifelong impact on the whole student. Experts accomplish this by focusing on each child, day after day, and focusing their Expert Lens on the long-range vision of Conceptual Mastery for all.

NOTE OF CAUTION

The examination of how experts plan and execute each element is necessary in visualizing the day-to-day functions in an expert's classroom. While the content is always in view and learning habits are constantly being developed, the expert shines in their day-to-day focus on developing each student's social-emotional attributes through rigorous learning experiences. The expert's classroom is one where all students feel supported and believe in their abilities to support their peers.

Experts' ability to focus on relationships is dependent on the deep level of understanding they have about content and pedagogical expectations. Due to their elaborate planning process, they are able to focus on developing students as a whole. Each day provides multiple opportunities for students to practice effective communication skills, show empathy toward their peers, or give and receive constructive feedback.

POINTS TO PONDER

- Experts create learning sequences of interconnected lessons to introduce, develop, refine, and reinforce thinking and learning.
- Experts match classroom structures to the learning tasks and to the needs of the students.
- Experts partner with students in all levels of learning to collect, analyze, and make choices based on evidence.
- Experts create engaging lesson sequences to develop the whole student.

Section III

BUILDING EXPERT CAPITAL

As an educational global community, we know what is needed for every student in every classroom to have powerful learning experiences day in and day out. The single most critical element is not the curriculum, the textbook, or the assessments. The single most critical element is the teacher. This fact has been proven over and over again through research studies upon studies and through each person's experiences. Expert teachers make a difference.

If we know this simple fact, beyond a reasonable doubt, why do we not do a better job at creating schools where expert teachers are the norm rather than the outlier? There are many cultural and political barriers to this Utopia occurring, but primarily, the goal is extremely lofty and as a community, we have instead focused on what we believe will fix the issues quickly.

For fifty-plus years, various reform efforts have pushed every magic bullet solution available, spending billions of wasted dollars, and only minimally impacting students. What if our efforts focused on developing expertise in teachers and in leadership? The charge is a lofty one. Imagine a nation where every child, every day, in every class was taught by an expert teacher.

EXPERT CAPITAL

Hargreaves and Fullan (2012) introduced the concept of professional capital in teaching by describing three kinds of capital found in teachers. Two focus on the individual: human capital, which is the talent of the individual, and decisional capital, which is the wisdom and expertise to make sound judgments about learners. The first is innate and the second is cultivated over many years of experiences. The other is social capital, which is the collaborative power of the group.

Expert Capital is professional capital at expert capacity. Expert Capital illustrates the collaborative power of expertise. First, experts have extreme human capital. They have intuitive abilities that are highly suited for teaching. They have high levels of compassion for others. They are also highly intelligent and reflective. They are highly efficacious. These natural abilities are critical in the initial recruitment of teachers. The experts also develop expert decisional capital through their constant reflection on and refinement of their teaching. They may plan a lesson but have multiple avenues for that lesson based on their experience. This high engagement in the reflection and refinement is critical in their development.

Finally, experts have high levels of social capital; however, they prefer to collaborate within groups that push their development of their expertise and meet the needs of their current students and their perceived teaching weaknesses. Social capital is increased when participants bond and bridge. Bonding describes the connections developed within the group, such as a school, whereas bridging describes the connections developed outside the group, such as professional organizations.

Experts create their own professional learning communities through bridging with experts outside of their school. While this is fully supported in the social capital research as one means of development, bonding within their school is missing. This lack of bonding creates a barrier not only for the expert to learn from others but also for the expert to share expertise.

This third truth is difficult to overcome in the current constructs of schools and professional learning systems. To overcome it is the key to leveraging the Expert Capital already in our schools, rather than ignoring it, to create a system of expertise.

FOUNDATIONAL UNDERSTANDINGS

The final chapters are about creating such a Utopia; however, to conceptualize such a dream requires remembering what makes experts, experts. First and foremost, experts are motivated by Teacher-Student Kinship, the deep, familial relationships they have with their students. They develop this relationship so they can develop Whole Student Understanding, which allows them to establish and advance an ever-growing understanding of the whole student's needs, abilities, knowledge, motivators, and external pressures.

This Whole Student Understanding is critical to experts' ability to focus and refocus their Expert Lens through their elaborate planning and day-to-day teaching to find solutions to the issues that arise in a student's learning continuum. Everything is about the students in the experts' classroom and their specific needs.

Understanding the expert is critical when seeking to create learning communities conducive to expertise. Existing Expert Capital is a valuable resource leaders may not leverage to build and further develop the highly effective teachers and effective teachers in their schools.

Learning to leverage this resource is the secret to creating an educational Utopia.

SECTION III: THINKING QUESTIONS

- What is the purpose of professional learning at your school?
- What is the purpose of professional learning for you personally?
- How would students be impacted if everyone on your campus was focused on developing Expert Capital?

Chapter 9

Expert Capital within Schools

In the ongoing exploration of expert teachers, the focus on professional learning of expert teachers has produced interesting conclusions about their needs, their actions, and the inadequacies of current professional learning models to meet their needs. The evidence led to several conclusions about the professional learning needs of expert teachers.

Expert teachers seek and find or create high-functioning professional communities with other experts to meet their professional learning needs. If their school meets their professional learning needs, they will engage and possibly lead in the school's professional learning community, in addition to their private learning communities. If the school's professional learning is inadequate in meeting their needs, the experts will "play the game" and quietly participate but will lean primarily on the support of their private professional community.

Experts make their professional learning choices based on the context of their students' needs and/or the specific needs they see in their teaching. Experts use evidence to make decisions inside and outside of the classroom. When they find an issue, they seek ways to help students overcome the issue in real time.

Experts recognize that encounters between other teachers and students are a resource for additional evidence about the student; however, they are often hesitant to ask teachers about their work with students. Part of the fear is the other teacher may perceive this as the expert questioning teaching skills or bring about negative consequences for the student. Experts often do not trust other teachers based on past interactions and comments they have witnessed from the teachers.

Additionally, many professional development activities in districts and schools are inadequate as there is a lack of focus on specific students' needs.

For example, a district notes vocabulary scores are low on the state assessment. The district purchases a vocabulary practice program and requires all students to practice thirty minutes a day. Teachers must sit through a session to learn how to use the program. This runs completely counter to expertise. The expert is more interested in understanding why vocabulary is an issue and if broad evidence supports this conclusion.

Experts also choose professional learning directly related to their perceived weaknesses in content, pedagogy, or social-emotional attributes. They seek to improve their weaknesses to improve student learning. For example, if a teacher believes her ability to teach writing is not at the expert level, she may join a National Writing Project program at the local university during the summer. When seeking to understand their perceived weaknesses, the expert appreciates being observed by other experts to discuss what may be happening in the lesson.

Expert teachers can and will function at high capacity regardless of school culture, but experts prefer an optimal school culture that supports strong professional learning communities. When experts are part of a subpar culture, they will often create small partnerships with other experts or highly effective teachers at their grade level or subject area. They will work to formally partner with these teachers such as creating interdisciplinary teams or moving to be next door. If optimum school culture is not an option, they will create these mini-cultures for themselves and their students.

Finally, transformational leadership is the preferred style of experts. They desire to be pushed, encouraged, understood, respected, and above all trusted by their leadership. When a leader is such a person, experts will recruit their expert and highly effective peers to apply for positions at the school. When the leadership is transactional, the expert will resist up to a point. For example, if a leader forces experts to perform at subpar levels through such elements as scripted lessons or rote-style programs, they will leave their schools for a school more conducive to expertise.

PROFESSIONAL LEARNING COMMUNITIES

Hipp and Huffman (2010, 12) describe professional learning communities as "professional educators working collectively and purposefully to create and sustain a culture of learning for all students and adults." Nonexperts focus on the word learning and connect the word to content mastery as measured by a test score. For nonexperts, professional learning is about raising test scores, school performance scores, and, in recent years, the value-added score of the teacher. They see professional learning as a way to find ways (how) to solve a problem as defined by a test score. Their "how" involves quick-fix strategies, test prep programs, and checking off mandates such as response to intervention.

Experts focus on the word learning and connect it to Conceptual Mastery of the whole student. For the experts, professional learning is about improving their practice to directly and specifically meet the needs of the whole student in order for each and every student to develop Conceptual Mastery. Experts seek professional learning based on the *why* behind the issues, before seeking solutions.

Experts understand that student learning will not improve without the teaching of learning and practice also improving. Experts collect wide arrays of evidence, analyze, and evaluate these pieces to understand why an issue exists, and then they seek solutions. Experts do not use quick fixes but rather access their private professional learning peers, read, explore options, and then try solutions through action research to refine and create solutions that work within their context.

Therein lies a critical difference leadership must recognize. Experts process specifically and slowly with great focus on the issues of their students. Their private professional learning groups they create are open, trusting, respectful, curious, and reflective. The members are all focused on the vision of Conceptual Mastery of the Whole Student. To create a professional learning community where expertise is consistently developed within a school requires the same vision from all members. Creating these types of relationships is possible when schools purposefully develop a strong culture of professional learning based on the five dimensions: (1) Shared and Supportive Leadership, (2) Shared Values and Vision, (3) Collective Learning and Application, (4) Shared Personal Practice, and (5) Supportive Conditions (Hipp and Huffman 2010).

Shared and Supportive Leadership

School administrators participate democratically with teachers by sharing power, authority, and decision making, and by promoting and nurturing leadership among staff. (Hipp and Huffman 2003, 29)

Trust begins when leadership and peers recognize that experts and their expertise exist. Recognizing expert teachers takes a deeper examination of a classroom than a simple observation of the teacher's words and actions. The secret to recognizing experts is to watch and listen to their students, both inside and outside of the classroom. Then, listen to the teacher reflect on the lesson. The teacher's focus will be on a wide range of evidence from the obvious concerning how many students were successful with whatever task to the subtle evidence noted like how a child wiggled or tune-out based on a facial expression.

Leadership and peers must also understand that experts see themselves simply as educators on a continual journey of learning and growing. Shared and supportive leadership is described in basically two elements: (1) democratic participation through the sharing of power, authority, and decision-making; and (2) the promotion and nurturing of leadership among staff. Both elements hinge on a culture of mutual respect and trust between all learners in the school.

Democratic participation includes sharing of power, authority, and decision-making, both inside and outside of the classroom. Experts desire the power to participate in all aspects of their students' experiences at school. Experts go above and beyond to make sure their students' needs are met. Shared leadership to experts means having the power or access to the power to meet the needs of students.

Experts focus on building Teacher-Student Kinship above all else, particularly in the beginning of the course. This means sometimes they will ignore a uniform infraction, such as a missing belt, in order to get a student to successfully complete an exponential function problem. They will then work on dress-code compliance once the relationship is developed.

When their authority is eroded by those who shift the focus from developing the whole student to miniscule compliance issues, experts are frustrated. Experts do not create roadblocks for students to be successful but rather help tear these down. Experts seek the joint authority to manage behavior, particularly during the development of the relationships with the child.

Experts also seek shared decision-making focused on evidence and the needs of their students, which is why experts are so resistant to top-down mandates. Experts do not need to always have issues solved their way, but the solutions need to be student-centered and grounded in the evidence and in best practice. When possible solutions are chosen, experts willingly participate, but want the freedom to fail, reflect, share, and adjust elements with peers. This is often seen as insubordinate in subpar cultures, but this ability to wrestle with complex solutions is part of the process in developing expertise.

> *My principal really has very little idea what's been going on in my classroom yet she's constantly passing down mmm you know mandate for accountability and ah you know mandate, you got to do things this way on this day you know and not allowing us per se to think about the kids as such.* (Abby, middle school)

Experts seek strong transformational leaders who push them to continually develop as professionals and leaders. These types of leaders allow the experts to grow and to share without alienating them among their peers. This element ties closely to Collective Learning and Application and Shared Personal Practice.

> *I have an awesome, incredibly supportive . . . mostly supportive principal who was in my classroom probably at least twice a week, interested in helping kids, working with kids, he knew what was going on in my classroom all the time. He loved to . . . to suggest; "Well why don't you go try this workshop?" or "Have you read this book?" and [he was] just incredibly supportive.* (Annie, middle school)

Shared Values and Vision

> *Staff shares values and visions for school improvement based on student needs and high expectations. Shared vision reflects norms and behavior that guide decisions about teaching and learning.* (Hipp and Huffman 2003, 39)

The expert's vision is for every student to achieve Conceptual Mastery through the development of the whole student. Any vision that is less than this exponential expectation is viewed as limiting and purposeless. The expert also has a set of deeply ingrained core values. When working on an instructional team, Amanda and her teammates created core values which they used to create a foundation of trust and respect on their team. These values served as a foundation for all decisions and a tool for resolving conflict. Their core values read as follows:

We believe. . .
 . . . the relationships we build with our students do not begin and end with the school day or the school calendar;
 . . . in a student-centered environment where all children feel safe and loved;
 . . . school should be an equitable place where all students have opportunities to succeed;
 . . . teaching students to take risks with their learning motivates them to tackle intellectual challenges throughout their lives;
 . . . learning should extend beyond the confines of our classrooms;
 . . . students must be actively engaged in learning so they will take ownership of their education and pride in class activities;
 . . . families are essential partners;
 . . . teachers should learn along with their students;
 . . . learning is a lifelong endeavor, and we are absolutely certain that every student can make a positive difference in the world. (Wild, Mayeaux, and Edmonds 2008)

Experts work toward a vision and their actions are guided by their deeply ingrained core values. When choices are made that run counter to the vision and/or the stated values of the group, experts flounder and lose trust. Many times schools have vision statements and state their values and beliefs, but then actions run counter. Experts are not swayed by words but rather examine evidence.

Collective Learning and Application

Staff at all levels of the school share information and work collaboratively to plan, solve problems, and improve learning opportunities. Together they seek knowledge, skills, and strategies, and apply what they learn to their work. (Hipp and Huffman 2003, 45)

Experts seek professional learning that is context-bound and will help them meet the needs of their students. When experts bring student work to a professional learning discussion with peers from the same content and who do not teach the same students, they are seeking evidence-based discussions about content issues. They want to examine the work through their Expert Lens, as well as others' Expert Lens to gain different perspectives. In this examination, they consider what was happening in the classroom while the work was being done, how the students reacted to the work, what questions students asked, and how they processed. This analysis is about figuring out why students are having an issue before reaching for a solution.

Experts understand their students are not simply in their classroom and their learning is multifaceted. They seek to understand the whole child and the whole of each issue, which requires a broad perspective, extensive evidence, and multilevel analysis. Experts recognize issues do not occur within the bubble of their classroom. Because experts have a deep representational understanding of their content, pedagogy, and social-emotional attributes, they make connections nonexperts do not.

One purpose for collective learning and application is to collect a wide array of evidence to better understand the whole student. The reason experts struggle with traditional professional learning activities is these are often segmented by content or by issues singled out by through a top-down mandate, rather than on the whole student.

For example, a student was struggling to understand what a lengthy word problem in math was asking. The student had struggled with the same issue for a few days. Her teacher, Mrs. Smith, asked the student to describe what she was visualizing in her mind as she read the problem. The student was clueless as to what the teacher was asking and was unable to visualize and make connections.

Mrs. Smith, a math expert, recognized there were some content issues, but suspected there was also a metacognitive issue with visualization and the ability to make connections. Before choosing possible solutions, Mrs. Smith met with the student's English teacher to see if the student was struggling to visualize and make connections in reading. The English teacher confirmed the student struggled often with these skills. The two teachers worked together to help the child through a series of strategies focused on developing her visualization skills and the ability to make connections.

The expert seeks additional information from other teachers to understand issues with learning habits. Optimally, all the teachers would work together to understand that not all issues are content-specific and strategies used in cross-curricular ways to help students overcome the issue in a more efficient manner.

Experts do seek to discuss content-specific issues with peers teaching the same content. The critical element is the focus is still on the whole student. The expert seeks to enhance their content-specific knowledge, skills, and strategies by working with content peers who teach different students. Experts also are willing to share their own expertise with content-specific peers, if the peers understand how the elements relate to the whole student.

Shared Personal Practice

Peers visit with and observe one another to offer encouragement and to provide feedback on instructional practices to assist in student achievement and increase individual and organizational capacity. (Hipp and Huffman 2003, 51)

Experts also enjoy sharing their practice when they feel safe to share their successes and their failures. Experts embrace failure as a learning tool, both with their students and in their own practice. Experts thrive when they are able to engage with other experts to increase their own knowledge, skills, and processes based on the needs of their students and their own perceived needs as a teacher. Experts do not seek observations of their teaching for validation but rather for refinement. They will often know where in their lesson there may be an issue and seek different points of view as to why the issue may be present.

Experts also enjoy breaking down a lesson and discussing the elements with others. When they are asked to mentor teachers, the expert understands the post-observation discussion is more critical than the observation.

Expert Vignette: Post-Observation Discussion

A few teachers observed Mrs. Bryant, an expert English teacher, during a lesson and then chatted with her during a post-observation discussion.

After the first English class, Mrs. Bryant made a quick adaptation in the order of the texts for the second class based on her observations during the lesson. The second group of students was more engaged and successful in achieving the target.

Afterward, one of the teachers asked Mrs. Bryant why she had made the change, to which she replied, "They were confused in the first class. I realized the second text allowed them to engage quickly and build confidence. So, I decided to test my theory and have them read it first."

The observing teacher asked, "But, how did you know that. None of them said they were confused."

Mrs. Bryant replied, "I read their facial expressions and body language while they were reading. Then I asked a few why they struggled with the first text and not the second."

The teacher looked at Mrs. Bryant quizzically and said, "I don't understand what that told you."

Mrs. Bryant responded, "Well, their knitted eyebrows indicated they were struggling. Mike and Lisa kept breathing hard and blowing out to show they were exasperated. When they got to the second text, they all calmed down and stopped fighting the text as hard. So, I asked a few questions and decided to see if the second text would work better in the beginning. It did."

Experts need to share their processing and explain why they made the decisions like they did. Post-observation discussion is beneficial in understanding the processing of the expert.

Supportive Conditions

Collegial relationships include respect, trust, norms of critical inquiry and improvement, and positive, caring relationships among students, teachers, and administrators. Structures include a variety of conditions such as the size of the school, proximity of staff to one another, communication systems, and the time and space for staff to meet and examine current practices. (Hipp and Huffman 2003, 57)

Collegial relationships are critical to experts to truly engage in professional learning. Much like experts create a strong culture of learning in their own classrooms, they expect the same type of culture in their schools. Experts will always care for their students and the needs of their students above all others in the school building. Understanding this element is key to understanding how to build relationships with the expert.

Experts seek others who believe in and focus on students. Experts willingly engage and participate in relationships with others who enjoy teaching and learning. Experts will share their expertise with leaders and teachers who are open with their own learning. Experts seek relationships to care for others and to be cared for by others.

Experts will not engage in relationship-building in a school where students are categorized and constantly targeted. Experts will not seek relationships with peers, who complain about students, berate and sabotage peers, and undermine leadership. Experts will not build relationships with leaders who are disorganized, disconnected, and do not demonstrate caring for students, teachers, and staff.

Finally, experts see supportive structures as evidence of proof of the value placed on professional learning. If professional learning is a stated value of the school, but no time is allocated for such, the expert will not trust this is a value. If teachers are pulled from professional learning to cover classes, the expert will view professional learning as not valued. If all professional learning is designed to meet top-down mandates or only focus on test scores, experts will simply disengage.

Leveraging Expert Capital

The experts' professional learning needs are very similar to the learning needs of students. They crave learning and successfully satisfy their craving either with or without their school community. Schools lose valuable capital when experts only increase their expertise through bridging outside of their school. To create powerful systems, existing Expert Capital must be successfully leveraged through both bonding and bridging.

Leveraging Expert Capital within a school to develop the expertise of all is dependent on two elements being met. First, experts desire strong professional relationships where they feel safe to reflect, share, and grow. Second, experts yearn for rigorous, high-quality learning experiences that make them think and deeply engage. Experts seek places to discuss the evidence of mastery they found in their classroom that day. They want to engage in collaborative peer observation structures and receive constructive feedback. They love to analyze student work for patterns and misconceptions with peers. Yet they are often hesitant to engage in any of these, because above all they need their peers and leadership to have and demonstrate the same heart for students and the same vision of success.

NOTE OF CAUTION

Experts will bond with peers within the school when the professional learning is student-centered and of high quality. However, experts will also continue to bridge with peers outside of their school, districts, and even states. Experts are consistently seeking to learn from other experts, which means they have an ever-growing network of peers from which they draw new knowledge and wisdom. Sometimes, this fact can be intimidating to peers within the school and to school leaders. To hinder the expert's need to bridge is to hinder their growth, which will also hinder the development of Expert Capital. Wise school leaders should work with experts to leverage these diverse networks to further develop the expertise of all.

POINTS TO PONDER

- Experts seek deep professional learning experiences focused on the needs of their students.
- Experts seek professional learning experiences with both teachers teaching the same students and teachers teaching the same content.
- Expert Capital is built when professional learning communities are strongly grounded in shared and supportive leadership, shared values and vision, collective learning and application, shared personal practice, and supportive conditions.
- Experts both bond with professionals within the school and bridge with professionals outside of the school.

Chapter 10

Professional Kinship

An examination of the expert's classroom culture yields a powerful vision of what the expert desires in a professional community. Everything begins with building, developing, and sustaining relationships. Experts create Teacher-Student Kinship with their students to understand the whole student and allow them to focus their Expert Lens on Conceptual Mastery of the whole student. Experts seek a similar type of relationships, what we will call Professional Kinship, within their professional learning communities.

Professional Kinship is an almost familial professional relationship experts create with leaders and peers, who also develop Teacher-Student Kinship with students. This collective understanding about how relationships are at the center to accomplishing the overarching vision for each and every student is foundational in developing strong professional relationships.

Experts recognize a student's experiences within the school day are not limited to the expert's classroom. Collaborating with teachers who work with the same students creates opportunities for the expert to develop a deeper understanding of the whole student through shared evidence and discussions. Additionally, when experts work with peers in collaborative teams, students benefit from a shared vision, common structures, and cross-curricular strategies.

Experts also recognize they are unable to continually refine their Expert Lens in isolation. While experts often have natural talent toward teaching, moving from effective and highly effective to an expert level benefits from critical conversations with peers. Deep, rigorous collaboration is critical to continual deep learning. However, the required level of collaboration can only occur in a deeply developed relationship where experts feel safe to use their expert processing collaboratively.

Professional Kinship, like its Teacher-Student twin, is grounded in respect, trust, efficacy, and perseverance. Experts seek strong relationships between all learners in the community, because, ultimately, these relationships benefit their students.

RESPECT

Respect is multifaceted. Experts deeply respect their students as humans and as learners. Experts evaluate the respect of peers and leadership based on how they interact with and about students. Experts will not develop relationships with adults who speak with bias against certain students or judge students. Experts will also not develop relationships with leaders who are disrespectful of students or the adults in the building. Experts are transformation people and expect leaders and peers to be transformational.

Respect is developed when all adults believe and demonstrate through words, actions, and beliefs in the shared vision of every student achieving Conceptual Mastery through the continual development of the whole student. Anything less is viewed as lack of respect for the student as a human, and therefore a lack of respect for the vision.

Additionally, respect is demonstrated when the values of the school are aligned with the vision as a basis for decision-making about everything from structures to schedules. For example, a demonstration of respect would be when leaders work collaboratively to create class schedules early enough for teachers to engage with students before classes begin. This simple example demonstrates respect for how experts build relationships with students prior to school beginning.

Experts are evidence-oriented people. Experts also judge respect on how evidence is used to make decisions. Experts consistently demonstrate expertise through concrete evidence. Respect is shown by acknowledging and using evidence to make decisions. Experts' level of respect in the school culture is directly impacted by how their work is acknowledged and used by peers and leadership.

TRUST

As previously discussed in relationship to Teacher-Student Kinship, trust is defined as "willingness to be vulnerable to another based on the confidence that the other is benevolent, honest, open, reliable, and competent" (Tschannen-Moran 2014, 19–20). In the discussions with experts, trust is often missing in their relationships with their peers and with leadership.

Developing the trust of an expert is to align values, actions, and words with the vision of the whole student being successful. Experts trust other educators who develop Teacher-Student Kinship with students and who work to achieve the overarching vision.

COLLECTIVE EFFICACY

Achieving Professional Kinship is dependent on the professional learning community's strong collective efficacy, which is the shared belief of the group's abilities to achieve the vision (Bandura 1997). For experts, this vision is for every student to achieve Conceptual Mastery.

Experts are highly efficacious about their abilities in their classroom. Experts' strong self-efficacy has been primarily developed through mastery experiences in teaching students. In their optimal professional learning, they seek to work with others, who are also highly efficacious about their teaching abilities. Additionally, experts bonding together results in enhancement of self-efficacy levels through vicarious experiences within the expert group. Yet strong individual self-efficacy does not automatically create strong collective efficacy in a group.

Rather, the collective efficacy of the group is built over time as the group works together to create optimal learning experiences for students, refine the teaching practices of the members of the group, and to overcome obstacles. Experts seek groups where their expertise is not only trusted and respected but also challenged.

Experts may or may not have high self-efficacy toward their abilities to develop expertise in others. This may partially be true due to lack of opportunity to work with effective and highly effective peers in their development toward expertise. In order to develop powerful Professional Kinship, each member of the learning community must believe in their individual abilities to impact peers' development toward expertise.

PERSISTENCE

Experts like challenging issues and obstacles, traditionally difficult to overcome. Experts seek and welcome new challenges and will persist to overcome the obstacles despite initial failure. Leveraging their determination to persist, in the face of all odds, is a powerful tool leaders can use to find unique solutions to difficult issues. Additionally, experts recognize obstacles are solved more efficiently when peers work together. Developing strong Professional Kinship relationships creates stronger persistence efforts as peers work together to create plans of action, reflect and refine these plans together, and push through difficult issues to achieve the vision.

Developing Professional Kinship

Roberts and Pruitt (2003) identify five stages of the change process that professional learning communities experience: forming, storming, norming, performing, and adjourning. Through these stages Professional Kinship is developed. However, not every professional learning community (PLC) will attain this level of relationship if individuals are not truly engaging in the process.

In the book *Teamwork: Setting the Standard for Collaborative Teaching* (2008), Amanda, along with her coauthors, Wild and Edmonds, describes the specific actions their team took within the process of developing Professional Kinship. These actions were focused on building an interdisciplinary team but are applicable to any PLC working toward Professional Kinship.

The formation of a PLC is often determined by arbitrary elements such as the class schedule. Experts form a PLC based on one purpose, meeting the needs of students. Experts may form a PLC to focus on specific content areas, but also see value in forming a PLC with interdisciplinary partners to focus on the whole students.

In the elementary and middle school levels, interdisciplinary teams easily fit to accomplish this task. These types of professional learning communities are also present at the high school level in First Year Academies. Strong interdisciplinary teams focus on the whole student and manage not only content development but also the development of learning habits and social-emotional attributes.

In the high school, interdisciplinary teams are more difficult due to the wide range of courses students take; however, PLCs can be formed based on moving the whole student toward a specific goal. An example will be shared in the next chapter. The major difference is the PLC is focused on the whole student rather than single test scores.

In the storming stage, groups begin to build trust and sort through the area of conflicts. This stage is where Professional Kinship begins to take root. Team-building activities that focus on defining strengths and weaknesses of the individual, such as Compass Points (see Suggested Resources), help members to understand one another and what each member needs to be productive and feel trusted and respected. The group also must develop the foundational elements upon which the norming will take place. Developing a set of core beliefs (values) is critical to understanding the vision of the team. Further development of practical elements such as procedures and expectations can also positively develop relationships.

Norming occurs early in the relationship-building process as the core beliefs, procedures, and expectations begin to work in real time. When members follow the agreed-upon norms with high fidelity, Professional Kinship begins to grow. Experts are always focused on students and their needs. When the group is focused on students and their needs and each member demonstrates commitment to this focus by attending to the norms set up by the group, Professional Kinship begins to grow.

Performing as a group to reach the vision is dependent on the strength of the relationships within the group. The actual Collective Expert Processing (performing) is the focus of the next chapter. As the group's abilities become more and more cohesive and effective, experts will seek more and more difficult challenges for the group. Experts will also tend to operate in more than one group, if their students or the expert has additional needs the group is not supporting. This is where an expert may bridge outside of the school to join professional organizations or form an expert group to focus on one issue.

Adjourning is a difficult stage for experts who have been engaged in successful, long-term Professional Kinship relationships. Experts who experience this type of collaboration are hesitant to move to another group, because they recognize creating the same level of relationship is time-consuming and difficult. When adjourning must occur, leadership should be cognizant of the impact it will have on the expert.

Finally, anytime a new member is added to a group, everyone has to go through the process of reforming. This is a difficult, but a critical, element if the group is to truly achieve Professional Kinship. A new member brings in new beliefs, new skills and talents, and new ideas.

NOTE OF CAUTION

Rather than seeing professional learning as a way to "teacher-proof" schools or manage learning from the top-down, true professional learning occurs from the ground level up, classroom by classroom, in schools where experts are recognized, purposefully developed, and utilized to lead others toward expertise. Two types of direct assaults will completely erode Professional Kinship for the expert. The first is an assault on Teacher-Student Kinship and the second is an assault on their Expert Lens.

When the experts' Teacher-Student Kinship is assaulted in such a vile manner, the experts struggle to regain trust. Assaults on Teacher-Student Kinship may be as simple as other teachers allowing students to watch movies every day, instead of teaching, to the school's administration interrupting a lesson to call students to impromptu assemblies or activities.

Regardless of the level of perceived transgression, experts lose trust, because students were not the focus of the adults. However, the most devastating assault is when students are purposefully treated unfairly by adults in the school and the adults' behaviors are not only accepted but also supported.

Actions that erode trust will have long-term impact on the professional learning community in a school and particularly on the expert.

Expert Vignette: Eroding Trust

Abby, a middle school teacher, shared her story.

I worked with this teacher, who was known to purposefully torment students, especially those with behavior issues. She would stand at her door and loudly point out dress code violations as students walked down the hall. She began targeting one of my most difficult students and after several days, the student reacted negatively. The peer immediately sent the student to the office. I was upset and felt the student had been targeted, so I requested a meeting with this teacher and our principal to discuss the issue. In the meeting she explained the only reason "those bad kids" behaved in my class was because I was weak on things like dress code. She felt it was her duty to punish my students.

Despite my protests, the student was suspended and I was told to not worry about students when they were not in my classroom. When the student returned to school, I began meeting the student at the bus every morning to check her for dress code adherence and walk her to class. After a few weeks, the administrator called me into his office to say my actions were unprofessional and were alienating my peers. I was not surprised by the other teacher's actions, but my administrator's complete inability to focus on the well-being of the student devastated me. I never could get past this incident and trust him again. I eventually left the school.

Another devastating assault on Professional Kinship is when expertise is discounted despite overwhelming evidence. Experts' dedication to the constant development of their Expert Lens and the success their students achieve is critical to their continual growth as professionals. Experts struggle when schools continually claim issues exist for which experts have developed and implemented strategies proven to work. Further frustration exists when solutions are created outside of evidence and forces upon the expert.

Expert Vignette: Frustrations

Paul, a high school teacher, described his experiences:

My students' assessment scores are always the highest in the district and often among the highest in the state. As for behavior, I have written up one student in five years and that was for an unavoidable offense. My students' tardiness and absenteeism are the lowest in the school and I suspect the district. So I have evidence I am effective. Yet, I keep getting these crazy mandates that run counter to what creates success for my students.

Last week, we were sent a ridiculous computer program that was nothing but a fancy workbook drill and kill. The intention was to correct the students' issues with basic skills. My students do not have these issues. No one asks me what I do to get results, but everyone wants to tell me how to do the job better. I am not perfect and I have very specific areas I am trying to improve. When I asked for evidence of why the program would work, the leadership told me to just do it, because it is a mandate. I am not doing it. They can fire me, but I am going to do what I know works for kids until someone shows me evidence otherwise. If I stay quiet, close my door, I can survive and my kids will keep thriving.

Professional Kinship to Collective Expert Processing

Leadership must always remember Teacher-Student Kinship is the central motivation for everything experts do, including why they develop Professional Kinship with peers. What entices experts in engaging in Professional Kinship is what they gain that they can use to positively impact their students. Experts recognize peers have additional evidence to understanding the whole student.

Experts seek this evidence to create mastery learning experiences for their students. They also seek this evidence to improve their own expertise. Finally, experts engage with peers as a way to increase the expertise of peers, therefore increasing the odds of students having effective learning experiences in other classes. This is the purest form of expert processing, collaborative processing, across the whole school to positively impact the whole student.

NOTE OF CAUTION

Experts seek transparency. Professional Kinship is not quickly created through the use of a few team-building activities at the beginning of the year. Professional Kinship takes time to develop and grow. Experts see through surface-level activities. School leaders who are seeking to create a culture where Professional Kinship thrives must remember that experts require respect and trust, if they are to deeply engage. Neither are built instantaneously. Patience is key. If trust and respect are either not solidly developed or broken, experts will withdraw or leave. Focus on building trust and respect through transparent and rigorous discussions.

POINTS TO PONDER

- Professional Kinship hinges on respect, trust, collective efficacy, and perseverance.
- Shared core values are keys to strong Professional Kinship.
- Evidence should matter but often experts are shunned despite powerful results in developing the whole student.
- Experts must be recognized and support by leadership.

Chapter 11

Collective Expert Thinking Process

In chapter 5, Expert Teacher Thinking Process was discussed as it occurs within a single classroom. While a single expert teacher can make a tremendous impact on a student's life, profound impact can be made when experts collectively work together to solve issues that occur across content and classes for students. Grounded in strong Professional Kinship, Expert Capital can be leveraged to use the Expert Teacher Thinking Process to find innovative solutions to issues students are experiencing, while also further developing the expertise of all educators in the school.

Expert teachers process the learning continuum as a whole to understand the conceptual pieces needed for the whole child to succeed. These understandings go well beyond standardized assessment requirements and focus on developing the whole child. Elaborate Planning is used to carefully construct each piece of the learning continuum.

Through day-to-day instruction, experts collect and analyze evidence to develop and test strategies to benefit students' learning. They are adept at evaluating possible strategies while seeking and adding further evidence to evaluate the effectiveness of the strategies. This process and the sharing of this process is motivating to experts, because experts enjoy solving problems that impact student development toward Conceptual Mastery.

COLLECTIVE EXPERT TEACHER THINKING PROCESS

The Expert Teacher Thinking Process in a collective effort focuses on finding solutions for issues that go beyond a single issue in a given content. These solutions are innovative and require participation from the small group of teachers in an interdisciplinary team to possibly a whole school. When

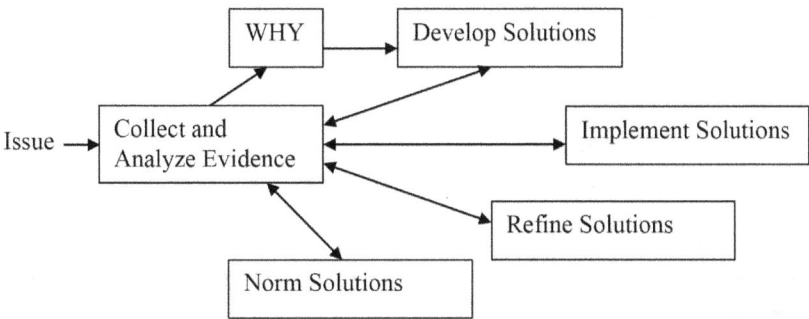

Figure 11.1 The Expert Teaching Thinking Process

experts engage in the highest forms of professional learning, the results can be quite remarkable.

Much like how the process occurs within a single classroom, the process remains consistent when a group works through it together. The differences are the evidence is much more comprehensive as it covers multiple classrooms and contents and the discussions are not simply between teachers and students but now engage other peers (see figure 11.1).

To visualize the process in action, the following example may prove useful to the readers.

Expert Vignette: Collecting Evidence

> Amanda was working in a middle school as an instructional leader, along with another instructional leader. They asked teachers to bring samples of assessments to the biweekly PLC meeting. Throughout the day, teachers analyzed their assessments for evidence of possible issues. After each group finished their analysis, she had them hang the assessments on the wall. By the end of the day, she had at least one assessment from each grade level and content.
>
> Amanda continued to look at these assessments and, as teachers stopped by, she would ask them if they saw any patterns. After a few days, she and another teacher realized if a question had any sort of attached stimuli (graph, table, map, political cartoon, etc.), the students either missed the question or skipped the question.
>
> Note the collection of evidence was the beginning of the process, rather than an analysis of standardized test scores. The issue is standardized test scores only tell teachers what students are missing, because the only evidence is a single number. This single number is not broad enough to understand what pieces students are missing and why. Additionally, a single number fails to yield information about where the misconception is

content-based, learning habit-based, connected to an interpersonal issue, or a combination.

Experts seek evidence to understand why misconceptions exist. When experts work collectively, they are able to explore even deeper into broader evidence for the connections or lack thereof students are making across content. This is particularly powerful when groups work to figure out metacognitive processes students are missing.

In this example, the evidence revealed two different issues. One, students were not able to analyze new information in the form of visual stimuli to make connections and inferences on assessments across content. Second, students demonstrated low self-efficacy when they encountered such questions, because they had connected their efficacy to only their ability to memorize and regurgitate information. The ability to analyze and process new information had not been developed.

Expert Vignette: Analyzing Evidence for the Why

> The group worked together to create a twenty-five-question pretest with questions with stimuli from all core contents. The pretest revealed only 23 percent of the students scored at the set level of proficiency, which was 75 percent. To further understand why the issue was occurring, Amanda met with small focus groups of students to ask them why these questions were difficult and why they had skipped them. The focus groups revealed students had the misconception that if they had never seen the particular stimulus, they were not able to answer the question. Therefore, students simply skipped the question or guessed.

The initial evidence only led to partial understanding of the why. The group created a tool, a pretest, to gather additional understanding and to set a baseline. The use of student focus groups led to a deeper understanding of how low self-efficacy was playing a role in the why behind the issue. This directly impacted how the group would implement the upcoming solution.

Expert Vignette: Developing Solutions

> Understanding the why led to a greater understanding of the issue. The students in the school had the misconception that assessments were only testing previously memorized knowledge, rather than higher-level skills such as being able to analyze new information to draw conclusions or making an inference from new information. Armed with this deeper understanding, Amanda and a small group of teachers developed a strategy to help students analyze new information that is presented as graphs, tables, maps, and political cartoons.

The development included a small group of teachers and Amanda working in pairs to understand what they did to analyze new information. One teacher took the pretest as another recorded what the teacher said and did for each question. The other pair did the same. Amanda observed and recorded. After they completed the process, they made connections and created a four-step process for analyzing any type of visual stimuli students may encounter.

Amanda pulled a group of five students and practiced the strategy with them. She recorded the sessions and then listened back to their responses and examined their work. Another teacher also observed and gave feedback. Once the strategy was ready to be used across the school, the group created a very specific structure for implementation. English teachers implement the strategy using charts and tables. Social studies teachers implemented the strategy using political cartoons and maps. Math teachers implemented the strategy with circle graphs, scatter plots, and histograms. Science teachers implemented the strategy with line, double line, and bar graphs.

Many professional learning community-style programs set up a structure where issues are found and solutions are chosen from a list of "best-practices" someone found. In fact, this school had such a program, which was very beneficial in many cases. Other issues had arisen during the year. The groups pulled already-existing solutions, including various standard strategies and implemented these with success.

However, Amanda was also working to help teachers learn to independently apply expert thinking in their classes. She created this experience to help them understand how to find why, how to engage peers and students in the process, and to teach them how to develop solutions when a standard did not exist.

The development she created was threefold. First, teachers actually did the work and unpacked the thinking, skills, and knowledge required. This not only developed their content knowledge but also helped them understand what students needed pedagogically and interpersonally. Then, the teachers analyzed what they had found to make connections in order to develop a solution, which in this case was the creation of an analysis strategy.

Finally, the strategy was practiced with a small group of students who worked with the teacher to give feedback and share their thoughts about the process. This final step allowed teachers to understand how to test and further develop solutions with student input.

Expert Vignette: Implementing and Refining Solutions

Implementation and refinement work hand in hand as experts refine solutions, both during implementation and after implementation. Over the course of three weeks, the strategy was implemented school-wide. Teachers modeled and students practiced the strategy. Peers, both teachers and students, observed and gave feedback.

Small focus groups of students were interviewed to measure the level of understanding. The group quickly realized the eighth graders were internalizing the strategy much quicker than the sixth and seventh graders, so many were allowed to use the strategy without concretely working through each step.

The implementation element has to be structured with expectations of teacher actions and classroom structures clearly defined. The evidence gathered for further reflection and refinement is dependent on the implementation being done in each room with fidelity.

After three weeks, a post-test was given to the students. The proficiency level was 93 percent and with students who were below proficiency scoring no lower than 65 percent correct on the test. This was a tremendous win for the students and for the teachers.

The critical element in the refining process is the engagement of students. This part of the process has the greatest impact on their self-efficacy, which as it increases, so does their perseverance. The students were equal partners in not only developing their own skills but also improving the skills of their peers. This success pushed students to understand assessments were not simply about memorized information but about learning to think and apply knowledge for deeper meanings.

For the teachers, they were overwhelmed that such growth could occur in such a short time frame. Had the solution only been applied in one classroom, those students would have improved, but they may have not transferred the strategy across content.

Norming Solutions

The strategy became a norm in the school with students using it effortlessly and intuitively as they encountered new information. The success also helped to build stronger Professional Kinship and further develop the teachers' lens toward an Expert Lens. The group moved forward to finding other issues in need of solutions.

Norming is a critical area often ignored as schools work toward solutions. For example, the stimuli strategy was mastered at each grade level within three weeks. Once mastered, the hope would be students would be able to go through the four steps without writing each one out every time they encounter new visual stimuli.

The steps were created to mirror the thinking processes highly efficient learners use, so true mastery would be the intuitive use of these steps. When schools choose strategies and continue to require students to write out each step, every time, year after year, the students are never required to internalize these as actually thinking processes. The norming of solutions into the learner's toolbox is evidence of Conceptual Mastery.

COLLECTIVE EXPERT THINKING IN SMALL GROUPS

The previous example was a school-wide example, but this process can also be applied within interdisciplinary teams, content-specific groups, and smaller groups with the same identified issue. In many states, the ACT test is a requirement for students to graduate from high school. Schools spend major money on test prep materials and software in efforts to increase scores. However, often the yield is minimal at best. Applying the Collective Expert Thinking Process has brought about increases in many schools.

Collecting Evidence

Amanda was working in a small rural district as an instructional leader, and then the school leader, when she began to consider the impact ACT had upon the students at the school. She analyzed the scores, which were very low and then set about to understand why. First, she took the test at her house and outlined what skills were required in each section. Then, she held discussions with focus groups of students to understand what they thought about each section and how they processed it. Then she observed what was happening in the classrooms.

As with the first example, the gathering of evidence is more than a single test score. The key to understanding why is to understand all of the complexities of the issue. In order to do so, experts collect a broad section of evidence from test scores to student experiences.

Analyzing Evidence for the Why

Amanda then analyzed all of the evidence and processed it with a peer from outside of the school. She then asked the teachers to work with her on analyzing the evidence. The findings showed a misalignment in what students were doing in school compared to what they had to do on the test. The analogy Amanda shares is, "We were teaching golf every day, but they were required to run a marathon."

The analogy explained part of why students were struggling. Similar to the middle school example, students shared they were "bad" at ACT and no matter how many times they took it, they could not improve. The teachers realized alignment was critical as never in a school day did students read a heavy chunk of cold text, then answer complex questions while being timed. The students seldom read and analyzed passages for grammar and punctuation. In math, they did not work a variety of cross-course problems for time. In science, they had never analyzed complex information and answered questions, again in a timed situation.

Developing Solutions

For each content, strategies and processes were created, which were focused on the needs of the student in that content. Teachers took their section of the test and worked through what students had to know and be able to do. They processed the restriction and the thinking requirements to create various solutions as issues arose. The teachers worked together when processes were similar, but each content had unique needs. The teachers then implemented their solutions through the bell-ringer time in each classroom.

Implementing and Refining Solutions

Over the course of six weeks, teachers worked independently with their students and collectively with peers to refine their solutions. Additionally, as student engaged and shared more evidence, more issues came to light. When the teacher could not find a solution, he or she would bring it to the group for an outside perspective.

Again, the critical element in the refining process is the engagement of students. When students are heard, they share more and they become more reflective. It also gives purpose to their learning, thus increasing engagement. The teachers were also focused on finding small issues within a larger issue, which helped develop their movement toward expertise.

Over the year, Amanda has continued to work with schools in developing solutions and strategies to help students with the skills and processes needed to be successful on ACT.

However, Amanda believes ACT is simply a vehicle to teach teachers and students to think like an expert about teaching and learning. The schools have had success with the process seeing their student move from proficiency percentage levels in the lower 30s to gains in the upper 70s.

Norming Solutions

The ACT has been part of Amanda's study of teachers and how they work independently and collectively toward expertise development. Despite the success, few schools continued the process in following years and scores returned to the lower levels. Outside of ACT, what we find is developing and sustaining a culture where the application of the Collective Expert Thinking Process is the norm is difficult. In part, this is due to teacher and leader turnover, a shift in focus for interventions, and simply lack of teachers willing to persist in this difficult process.

POINTS TO PONDER

- Solutions to any issue are possible when professionals use multiple points of evidence to understand *why* the issue exists and then work collectively and purposefully to find solutions.
- Solutions are not simple but require reflective implementation and refinement.
- Successful solutions are normed into the school culture to become part of the teaching and learning toolbox of all learners.

Final Thoughts

Instead of spending billions of dollars on new curricula, constantly changing standards and assessments, and more "stuff" to help students practice for tests, true reform centers all efforts and funding on recruiting, developing, refining, and retaining expert teachers in every classroom, in every school. The encouraging news is some classrooms are already led by experts and in others, there are highly effective teachers and effective teachers who can be nurtured to develop their expertise. Unfortunately, expertise is often misunderstood, overlooked, or, even worse, shunned.

Building a system focused on the development of the whole students requires a shift in the collective thinking. Leadership and policymakers must understand and recognize expertise is the unleashing opportunities for all students. Expert teachers are intelligent, passionate, and focused on the whole student.

They are highly motivated by strong Teacher-Student Kinship and constantly seek professional learning to further develop their Expert Lens. Experts plan and implement lessons using an elaborate system with multiple pathways they may access to help students achieve Conceptual Mastery. Experts prefer professional learning focused on this end goal and prefer to work with leadership and peers, who are equally focused on this end.

If the success of every student, in every classroom, in every school, is truly the goal, quick-fix efforts and checklist systems with teacher-proof guarantees must be eliminated. We also must recognize all of the dirty secrets from protecting ineffective to harmful teachers. Building an expert system will bring forth sustainable and powerful change for all students.

Appendix

Professional Learning Activities

EXPERT CAPITAL EXERCISE: SHARE AND SUPPORTIVE LEADERSHIP

The purpose of this exercise is to analyze the current perceptions of the professional learning community within the school. Findings should be used to make next-step decisions in improving areas of weakness and capitalizing on areas of strengths.

Step 1: Administer the Professional Learning Community Assessment-Revised (PLCA-R) to all members.
Step 2: Collect and analyze all data.
Step 3: Share data with members of the PLC.
Step 4: Choose one area of weakness to focus on improving for the year. Some initial activities are suggested in the following exercises.
Step 5: Throughout the year, monitor through broad-based evidence, refine, and reflect.
Step 6: At the end of the year, readminister the PLCA-R. Using the data and other evidence, make decisions about next steps.

SUGGESTED RESOURCES

PLCA-R (Olivier and Hipp, 2010, 32–35) can be found in Kristine Kiefer Hipp and Jame Bumpers Huffman. 2010. *Demystifying Professional Learning Communities*. New York: Rowman and Littlefield.

EXPERT CAPITAL EXERCISE: SHARED VALUES AND VISIONS

The purpose of this exercise is to develop shared values and visions by establishing a set of core beliefs statements for the school and/or each team. Core beliefs are used as a foundation for decision-making.

Step 1: Ask members to outline their reasons for becoming an educator. Suggested tool: Passions Profiles from National School Reform Faculty.

Step 2: Ask members to individually list what they believe about teaching and learning by responding to the following questions:

- What do you believe about your abilities as a teacher?
- What do believe about your abilities as a learner?
- What do you believe about students?
- What are your responsibilities as a teacher to the individual student? To your peers? To the school? To families? To the community?
- What does respect mean to you? How is respect established?
- What does trust mean to you? How is trust established?
- What are the responsibilities of the school to you? To your peers? To students? To families? To the community?

Step 3: Chart their beliefs based on the following statements:

- I believe school is. . .
- I believe my classroom is. . .
- I believe learning is. . .
- I believe students are. . .
- I believe families are. . .
- I believe my peers are. . .
- I believe leadership is. . .

Step 4: Using the information from Steps 2 and 3 begin to find consensus about what the team believes as a whole. A suggested structure to find consensus for each piece is Placemat Consensus (Bennett and Rolheiser 2001).

Step 5: After the core beliefs are developed, allow members to comment and suggest revisions, before finalizing the list.

Step 6: Integrate the Core Beliefs into discussions and actions throughout the year.

SUGGESTED RESOURCES

Bennett, Barrie, and Carol Rolheiser. 2001. *Beyond Monet: The Artful Science of Instructional Integration*, 172–3. Ajax, Ontario: Bookation.

National School Reform Faculty. "Passion Profile." https://www.nsrfharmony.org/wp-content/uploads/2017/10/passion_profiles.pdf

National School Reform Faculty. "Passion Profile Activity." https://www.nsrfharmony.org/wp-content/uploads/2017/10/passion_profiles_activity.pdf

EXPERT CAPITAL EXERCISE: COLLECTIVE LEARNING AND APPLICATION

The purpose of the following group of exercises is for the professional learning community to develop a school-wide working definition of Conceptual Mastery. Exercises will require members to work independently and then bring their analysis to the PLC for discussion.

Professional Learning Question: What is the definition of Conceptual Mastery the whole student?

Exercise 1 (Individuals): Each member should read their entire curriculum through from the last unit to the first unit. As they read, they will annotate knowledge, skills, and processes students will need to achieve content mastery.

Exercise 2 (Individuals): If available, members will complete the standardized assessment aligned to their curriculum. As they take the assessment, they should note knowledge, skills, and processes students will need to achieve content mastery. Members will analyze the test structure for directions, question structure, how answers are given, and any other non-content skills students need to be successful.

Exercise 3 (Content-Based Teams): Members work together in content groups to process their findings to describe Conceptual Mastery of their content.

How does the assessment define content mastery?
What overarching content knowledge, skills, and processes do students need to achieve mastery of the content?
What learning habits do students need to develop over the year to be successful?
What social/emotional skills do students need to develop over the year to be successful?
What is Conceptual Mastery of our content?

Exercise 4 (Interdisciplinary Teams): Members are reorganized to work with members who teach the same students. Members share individual curricular findings. How does the assessment define content mastery?

> What overarching content knowledge, skills, and processes are shared between our curricula? Examples follow: analyzing variety of stimuli, writing to explain thinking, or evaluating information to draw conclusions.
> What shared learning habits do students need to develop over the year to be successful?
> What shared social/emotional skills do students need to develop over the year to be successful?

Exercise 5 (Whole School): Members work together to create a definition that describes a student who has achieved Conceptual Mastery.

> What is Conceptual Mastery of the whole student?

EXPERT CAPITAL EXERCISE: SHARED PERSONAL PRACTICE

The purpose of this exercise is to create a culture where teachers are encouraged to share personal practice. Opening doors to classrooms is often a scary experience for teachers. Often when teachers are observed, the purpose is evaluation. Flipping this concept to where teachers view observations as opportunities to develop, share practice, and impact others is difficult. Opening doors in a positive manner is the first step. One idea is to host a treasure hunt where participants seek professional treasure.

Initial Treasure Hunt

Step 1: Create a huge treasure box on the wall of the professional learning center room or faculty room.
Step 2: Prior to school opening, assign teachers visit each other's classrooms to look for treasures (positive elements). Visitors will write down three to five examples of treasure.
Step 3: Post the sheets with the list on the treasure box for everyone to see.
Step 4: At the first PLC, have members reflect on the treasure found in their classrooms.
Align to the core beliefs by asking members how these pieces may be considered evidence of core beliefs in action.

Second Treasure Hunt

Step 1: During the first week of school, assign teachers to visit each other's classrooms to look for treasure that exemplifies teachers building relationships with students. Visitors will write down three to five examples of treasure.
Step 3: Post the sheets with the list on the treasure box for everyone to see.
Step 4: During the PLC, have members reflect on the treasure found in their classrooms.
Align to the core beliefs by asking members how these pieces may be considered evidence of core beliefs in action.

Future Treasure Hunts

Repeat the cycle but have observers find treasure for the specific topic and then pose a question or a what if for the teacher being observed. For example, if the observer's focus is student engagement, the observer may write:
The treasure I found is most students are engaged in the activity and the activity is aligned to the learning target.
What if the students worked in pairs, instead of groups of four? How would that increase engagement?

If there is a school-wide pattern observed in student engagement, then during the next professional learning opportunity, increasing student engagement may be the focus. The observation notes from everyone provide significant evidence.

The idea of finding treasure creates a positive spin on peers visiting classrooms for the purpose of learning and sharing personal practice. Obviously, expertise development requires deep and critical engagement, but building respect and trust is the first step. Using the ideas of treasure hunts in the beginning is one way of changing perceptions and planting the seeds for Professional Kinship to take root.

EXPERT CAPITAL EXERCISE: SUPPORTIVE CONDITIONS (RELATIONSHIPS)

This exercise is designed to assist teams in the early stages of development to understand each members' gifts and talents.

Step 1: Have members complete a personality survey. One easy and free tool can be found at www.16personalities.com.

Step 2: Ask individuals to analyze their results and write down their strengths, weaknesses, and what they need from others to work productively.

Step 3: The personalities are grouped in larger groups of four. Have the four groups come together to develop a list of their strengths, weaknesses, and needs.

Step 4: Share the lists with the groups as a whole.

Step 5: Allow teams to work together to develop team-wide procedures and expectations based on the strengths, weaknesses, and needs of the group.

SUGGESTED RESOURCES

National School Reform Faculty. "Compass Points Protocol." https://nsrfharmony.org/protocols/

https://www.nsrfharmony.org/wp-content/uploads/2017/10/north_south_0.pdf

Wild, Monique D., Amanda S. Mayeaux, and Kathryn P. Edmonds. 2008. *Teamwork: Setting the Standard for Collaborative Teaching: Grades 5–9.* Portland: Stenhouse.

Section I, Chapter 1: Learning to Work with Colleagues (11–31)

Expert Capital Exercise: Supportive Conditions (Structures)

The following are a list of suggested resources for creating structures conducive to developing Expert Capital.

References

Bandura, Albert. 1993. "Perceived Self-Efficacy in Cognitive Development and Functioning." *Educational Psychologist* 28 (2): 117–48.
Bandura, Albert. 1997. *Self-Efficacy: The Exercise of Control.* New York: Freeman & Company.
Berliner, David C. 2004. "Expert Teachers: Their Characteristics, Development and Accomplishments." In *De la teoria . . . a l'aula: Formacio del professorat ensenyament de las ciències socials*, edited by R. Batllori i Obiols, A. E Gomez Martinez, M. Oller i Freixa, and J. Pages i. Blanch, 13–28. Barcelona, Spain: Departament de Didàctica de la Llengua de la Literatura I de les Ciències Socials, Universitat Autònoma de Barcelona.
Costa, Albert L., and Robert J. Garmston. 2001 "Five Human Passions: The Origins of Effective Thinking." In *Developing Minds: A Resource Book for Teaching Thinking*, 3rd ed., edited by Albert L. Costa, 18–22. Alexandria, VA: Association for Supervision and Curriculum Development.
Covington, Martin V. 1998. *The Will to Learn: A Guide for Motivating Young People.* Cambridge: Cambridge University Press.
Csikszentmihalyi, Mihaly. 1990. *Flow.* New York: Harper Perennial.
Darling-Hammond, Linda, and Robert Rothman. 2011. "Teacher and Leader Effectiveness in High-Performing Education Systems." *Alliance for Excellent Education and Stanford Center for Opportunity Policy in Education.*
Darling-Hammond, Linda. 1995. *Professional Development Schools: Schools for the Developing a Profession.* New York: Teacher's College Press.
Good, Thomas L. and Jere Brophy. 2008. *Looking in Classrooms.* 10th ed. Boston, MA: Allyn & Bacon.
Hargreaves, Andy and Michael Fullan. 2012. *Professional Capital: Transforming Teaching in Every School.* New York: Teachers College Press.
Hattie, John A. 2003. "Teachers Make a Difference: What Is the Research Evidence?" *Australian Council for Educational Research* (October): 1–17.

Hattie, John A. 2010. *Visible Learning for Teachers: Maximizing Impact on Learning.* New York: Routledge.

Hipp, Kristine K., and Jane B. Huffman. 2003. *Reculturing School as Professional Learning Communities.* Lanham: Scarecrow Education.

Hipp, Kristine K., and Jane B. Huffman. 2010. *Demystifying Professional Learning Communities: School Leadership at Its Best.* Lanham, MD: Rowman & Littlefield.

Housner, Lynn D., and David C. Griffey. 1985. "Teacher Cognition: Differences in Planning and Interactive Decision Making between Experienced and Inexperienced Teachers." *Research Quarterly for Exercise and Sport* 56 (1): 45–53. doi: 10.1080/02701367.1985.10608430.

Hunter, Madeline. 1982. *Mastery Teaching.* Thousand Oaks, CA: Corwin Press.

Mayeaux, Amanda. 2013. *Motivating Teachers towards Expertise Development: A Mixed-Methods Study of the Relationships between School Culture, Internal Factors, and State of Flow.* Lafayette: University of Louisiana at Lafayette.

Rivkin, Steven G., Eric A. Hanushek, and John F. Kain. 2005. "Teachers, Schools, and Academic Achievement." *Econometrica* 73 (2): 417–58.

Roberts, Sylvia M., and Eunice Z. Pruitt. 2003. *Schools as Professional Learning Communities: Collaborative Activities and Strategies for Professional Development.* Thousand Oaks, CA: Corwin Press.

Rockoff, Jonah. 2004. "The Impact of Individual Teachers on Student Achievement: Evidence from Panel Data." *The American Economic Review Papers and Proceedings of the One Hundred Sixteenth Annual Meeting of the American Economic Association. San Diego, CA* 94 (2): 247–52.

Sanders, William L., and June C. Rivers. 1996. *Research Project Report: Cumulative and Residual Effects of Teachers on Future Student Academic Achievement.* Knoxville: University of Tennessee Value-Added Research and Assessment Center.

Shulman, Lee. 1987. "Knowledge and Teaching: Foundations of the New Reform." *Harvard Educational Review,* 57 (1) (February): 1–22.

Tschannen-Moran, M. 2014. *Trust Matters: Leadership for Successful Schools.* 2nd ed. San Francisco, CA: Jossey-Bass.

Venables, Daniel. 2011. *The Practice of Authentic PLCs: A Guide to Effective Teacher Teams.* Thousand Oaks, CA: Corwin.

Voss, James F., and Timothy A. Post. 1988. "On the Solving of Ill-Structured Problems." In *The Nature of Expertise,* edited by M. H. Chi, R. Glaser, and M. J. Farr, 261–85. Mahwah, NJ: Erlbaum.

Weisberg, D., S. Sexton, J. Mulhern, and D. Keeling. 2009. *The Widget Effect: Our National Failure to Acknowledge and Act on Differences in Teacher Effectiveness.* New York: The New Teacher Project.

Wild, Monique, Amanda Mayeaux, and Kathryn Edmonds. 2008. *Teamwork: Setting the Standard for Collaborative Teaching, Grades 5–9.* Portland, OR: Stenhouse Publishers.

About the Authors

Amanda Shuford Mayeaux, EdD, NBCT, is an assistant professor at the University of Louisiana at Lafayette in Educational Foundations and Leadership. She has worked in the field of education for almost three decades from classroom to leadership positions at various levels. Amanda's research interests include teacher expertise, experiences of gifted rural students and families, reduction of organizational barriers to student success, policy construction, and comprehensive training for emerging leaders. She has been a National Board of Professional Teacher Standards certified teacher since 2001. In 2003, she was named a Milken Family Educator and was the Disney Teacher of the Year and Disney Middle School Teacher of the Year in 2006. She is the coauthor of several publications, including *Teamwork: Setting the Standard for Collaborative Teaching, Grades 5–9*. Since joining the University of Louisiana at Lafayette, she has worked with aspiring school leaders in the graduate program, as well as sharing her teacher expertise with emerging teacher candidates in the undergraduate program. Amanda may be contacted at amanda.mayeaux@louisiana.edu.

Dianne F. Olivier, PhD, professor in Educational Foundations and Leadership at the University of Louisiana Lafayette, serves as Coordinator of the Doctoral Program and holds the Joan D. and Alexander S. Haig/BORSF Endowed Professorship in Education. She has received University honors for research excellence and outstanding doctoral mentorship. Dianne has served as chair for over sixty doctoral dissertations. Her research focuses on educational leadership, professional learning communities, school culture, and teacher self-efficacy and collective efficacy. She has developed several assessments and has authored/coauthored numerous chapters and journal articles relating to her research interests. Her PLC research has transitioned from twenty years at the domestic national level to a global perspective as a member of a Global PLC Network. She has been invited to conduct international presentations in Australia, Canada, Hong Kong, Indonesia, Ireland, Singapore, and Taiwan. Prior to the university level, Dianne served thirty-four years in public education, with twenty-six of those years as a district administrator. She uses her former K–12 administrative experiences to work throughout the United States with principals, central office personnel, and teacher leaders in her role as an educational consultant with the Learning-Centered Leadership Program for the Southern Regional Education Board. Dianne may be contacted at dianne.olivier@louisiana.edu.

www.ingramcontent.com/pod-product-compliance
Lightning Source LLC
Chambersburg PA
CBHW051813230426
43672CB00012B/2714